ALSO BY MARTHA FAY

A Mortal Condition

CHILDREN AND RELIGION

Making Choices

in a Secular Age

MARTHA FAY

A Fireside Book   Published by Simon & Schuster
New York London Toronto Sydney Tokyo Singapore

FIRESIDE
Rockefeller Center
1230 Avenue of the Americas
New York, New York 10020

First Fireside Edition 1994
Published by arrangement with Pantheon Books,
a division of Random House, Inc.

Previously published as *Do Children Need Religion?*
FIRESIDE and colophon are registered trademarks
of Simon and Schuster Inc.

Designed by Debbie Glasserman
Manufactured in the United States of America

1   3   5   7   9   10   8   6   4   2

Library of Congress Cataloging-in-Publication Data
Fay, Martha.
[Do children need religion?]
Children and religion : making choices in a secular age /
Martha Fay.—1st Fireside ed.
p.   cm.
"A Fireside book."
Originally published: Do children need religion? New York :
Pantheon Books, c1993.
Includes bibliographical references.
1. Children—Religious life.   2. Child rearing—Religious aspects.
I. Title.
[BL625.5.F388   1994]   93-45036
248.8′2—dc20   CIP

ISBN: 0-671-88582-0

FOR ANNA

Contents

Introduction

This book had its beginnings in a series of linked converations I had quite by chance several years ago with a handful of parents of young children. Some were close friends, some acquaintances, others strangers in the schoolyard or playground—but all of them confessed themselves surprised and somewhat bewildered by the sudden urgency of a question that had completely failed to attract their interest previously: Do children need religion?—or more pertinently: Does *my* child need religion?

It was a question that demanded more than a simple answer, and that laid bare the reality of how changed our current circumstances were from the conditions in which most of us were raised. Sometime between our own childhoods and the present, the world and much that we took to be fixed in it had shifted. The moral and cultural landscape in which we lived and in which we were now raising children was, we knew, vastly different from that of our own childhoods. Yet our hopes for our children—that they become good and loving people, that they find a place in the culture, that they know where, as one parent said, they "fall in history"—were not so different from the long-ago hopes our parents dutifully or devoutly shored up with organized religion. How, we were suddenly asking ourselves, did we get here from there? And what is it that our children require of religion?

Since then, I have many times found myself staring at an unframed photograph of my family taken when I was about the age my daughter is now. It shows my parents and six of their eight children arranged in a devotional semicircle around a coffee table, all of us on our knees and saying the rosary, as we did every night. In the background stands a statue of Our Lady of Fatima, which my father had brought back from a trip to Portugal he had made in 1950. I can recall precisely how it felt, elbows and knees braced for the duration. It is harder to resurrect the serene and certain state of mind it captures.

It is a picture not just from another time but from another world, and it has its equivalents in the picture boxes, or memories, of the majority of the people I have interviewed: choir practice, church picnics, Bible summer school, Hebrew classes, heads bowed in prayer in public school assemblies and before the big game. In the world in which most of us grew up, religious doubt and religious errancy were, like marital infidelity and parental despair, matters to be kept secret from the children.

Everyone our family knew was something—Catholic or
ex-Catholic, Protestant or Jew, benighted or misguided,
but all *something*—all *nameable,* and thus explainable. By
the time I finished college, in 1968, that world had broken
apart and most of the people I knew, having jettisoned
the religious identity they had grown up with, were emphatically *not* something. One's childhood religion, my
own included, was part of one's story but it was only
rarely part of one's present.

Some seventeen years later, when my own young
daughter began inquiring about metaphysical matters, I
could not have accounted for the religious backgrounds
of the majority of my friends (apart from the ex-Catholics
whom I seem to have attracted in some disproportion).
With only a few exceptions, I was similarly unaware, for
example, of anyone having conjugal disputes over
whether to baptize or circumsize their newborn infants.
Friends of mine who were having their first babies in their
mid-thirties talked incessantly about childbirth classes,
whether or not to continue working, the problems and
terrors of day care, of apartments too small or spouses
too reluctant, but they did not talk about their spiritual
plans for their children.

Thus when I first began to raise the subject with
friends, I was unprepared for the flood of self-accusation,
nostalgia, regret, guilt, and fantasy it released, even
among those few who appeared to have settled the question. The issue of religion—of belief, of observance, of
tradition, and the desire or reluctance to pass it on—had
not disappeared but simply gone underground, to become, it seemed, the last unshared secret of our extraordinarily confessional generation.

As in my own case, the catalyst for reflection for most of the people I talked to had been parenthood, and what nagged at the consciences of these loving, if slightly novice, guardians was fear of what a lack of religion might somehow do to their children. If they failed to offer their children some form of religious instruction, were they simply leaving the door open for a choice to be made later in life, or were they slamming it shut forever? It was far easier to invoke the reasons why children should be given religion: because it provides answers to their questions about the world, about life and death; because it offers a moral or ethical code; because it satisfies their need for order and security; because it coincides with their magical fantasies; because it makes them members of a spiritual community; because it teaches them that there is something bigger and more important than their own individual concerns.

What they themselves believed, on the other hand, was so idiosyncratic and personal as to defy categorization.

There were nonbelievers who thought a belief in God and some form of religious training were salutory things to give children, as well as believers who held that organized religion was organized hypocrisy. From those who had grown up without religion, I heard everything from regret to gratitude to bewilderment, and I heard precisely the same things, with only incidental alterations, from those who had grown up with it. Some who had had the benefit of a conventional religious upbringing seemed nevertheless to be considering its meaning for the first time and found themselves deeply unsettled, while for others, religion was simply one of the duties of adult life, and especially of parenthood—like taking on the re-

sponsibility of a mortgage or making dental appointments. For still others, it remained so emotionally charged
an issue that they had simply never been able to focus on
it—sometimes because of childhood experiences, sometimes because of the seeming impossibility of coming to
agreement with a spouse from a different background.
The most regular churchgoers were, predictably, the least
confused about why they went and why they took their
children: because they felt that it established a moral center
for their lives, and because they could not imagine life
without belief. But even among this group, apart from
a basic conviction that there must be a God, and for
Christians the further conviction that Jesus was divine,
theology and doctrine counted for little as compared to
a private sense of rightness—or sometimes just the quality
of the music.

Catholics went to mass when they wanted to, practiced
birth control without a second thought, and exhorted
their children to good behavior not with threats of hell
but in a manner indistinguishable from that of secular
humanists. Protestants switched denominations or parishes as readily as they traded in their old cars, and with
greater regard for political ideology than theology.
Among Jews, the gradations of belief and practice were
even more pronounced, with the dual nature of Judaism
as both religion and culture making it possible—possibly
even mandatory—for every Jew to construct his or her
personal Jewish identity out of a long list of available
options and absolutes.

In fact, the more I heard, the more obvious it became
that there exists little common understanding of what we
mean by religion. Is it belief in a God or a set of beliefs

about how we are to behave? A willingness to worship in community or a private conviction? Is it ceremony and ritual or a conceit of deference to the unseen and unknowable? Or is it, particularly given the death of creed, primarily an accident of birth and culture, continued from one generation to the next until some new fact forces a reconsideration that in turn prompts a fresh choice?

This book does not attempt to cover the full spectrum of religious sentiment or religious practice. It does not take up the issue of fundamentalism, nor does it linger long on those who are happily unconfused on the subject of religion. It is primarily an exploration of the muddle in which a large number of people unexpectedly find themselves by virtue of becoming parents: the obligation to think about what they believe and how they wish to transmit those beliefs to their children in a time when such an obligation is easily sidestepped.

For a large part of the generation of Americans who came of age in the 1960s and 1970s, the automatic continuance of the religion of their childhood turned out to be difficult or impossible for a number of reasons. The ecumenical movement, for example, though its admirable aim was to put an end to denominational jealousies, proved even more successful in persuading many of the faithful that one religion is as valid as another. More or less simultaneously, and just as abruptly, it seemed, interest in non-Western cultures and religions blossomed among the young with an intensity not seen in earlier generations. America, and especially the press, was fixated on cults and their dangers, as it would later become fixated on the more significant resurgence of fundamentalism and, more recently, an apparent revival of conventional churchgoing. For most people, however, the consequence of these many influences was not an immediate conversion to some new vision but something more subtle, having to do with the realization that the certainties of the past were anything but certain.

Even more powerful as an agent of disaffection, however, has been simple demographics. As more and more of the postwar, or "baby boom," generation did exactly what young Catholic schoolchildren were warned against from the earliest grades—namely, marry outside the religion of their parents—the possibilities for a natural continuity of faith, or even a continuing conviction about there being one true path to follow, diminished.

Though one assumes marriage between people of different backgrounds to be more common today than for previous generations, it was only after I started making lists of interview subjects and their backgrounds that I realized how much it had become the rule rather than the exception. It was as if we had all been engaged in a mating version of musical chairs in which there was little chance of winding up with the boy or girl from next door—and especially not with anyone from the next pew.

Only after the first baby arrived did we begin to comprehend how powerfully religion had helped shape who we were, and that a choice of some kind might have to be made. To many people who had given it no thought earlier, it suddenly seemed *not* all right to be nothing, and again and again over the last several years I have heard expressed the conviction—for some it would be more correct to say the anxiety—that every child needs to be so named and so situated in time and history and culture.

"Going to Sunday school," said one father who expressed serious reservations about the value of organized religion, "is still culturally appropriate in this society. That is why I don't object."

"I want him to feel that sense of awe I felt as a child," said one mother who was greatly opposed to organized religion. "But I have no model for it other than religion."

And another father: "I want her to know where she falls in history."

Whatever choice any of us makes privately, by definition our children live in a secular age, in a country deeply tied to the habit of religion, and as deeply conflicted about its meaning. America, Harold Bloom remarks several times over in *The American Religion,* "is a religion-mad country. It has been inflamed in this regard for about two centuries now." Americans believe in God and attend church in far greater numbers than almost any of the countries from which its people derive, and our faith is expressed in more than a thousand different denominations. To describe what any of these actually holds to be true or central, Bloom observes, is nearly impossible. Religion in America is primarily a personal quest, and it has made us a country of spiritual transients: while some 80 percent of all American adults claim membership in a religious congregation, close to a third say they have belonged to the same congregation for fewer than five years, while another 20 percent claim even shorter membership. And increasingly, the choice of a church to belong to is a choice made in isolation, independent of family ties or community.

"Religion plays a very different role now than it did 50 or 100 years ago," observes Randall Balmer, whose *Mine Eyes Have Seen the Glory* explores the evangelical world of his childhood. "It used to explain the natural world. Now, for most people, it no longer does. Instead it has to do more and more with issues of personal well-being, forcing it to compete with psychotherapy and other newer alternatives." So difficult are these expectations to fulfill, said one minister, that it actually comes as a relief when new parishioners say they have come for their children's sake. That, at least, is a purpose he can hope to address.

For many people, parenthood does in fact constitute the most powerful motivation for dealing with the immensely complicated question of religious practice and belief. To tell one's child what one truly believes requires a degree of honesty and a capacity for self-revelation that goes well beyond the ordinary demands of caretaking and affection. To take full responsibility for one's children's moral and religious instruction, moreover, requires a sense of personal legitimacy that is sometimes hard to summon, and can hardly be guaranteed. In giving one's child a religious upbringing, one enjoys the sense that one has done the right thing and taken a well-known road. In choosing not to give one's child a religious upbringing, one takes a position of another sort, setting them on a path many of us did not discover until much later in our lives.

"At a certain point," said Jerry Delaney, a father who himself had been raised in a warring Protestant-Catholic household, "all three of my daughters expressed anger with me that they weren't given a faith when they were young. And my answer to all of them was, 'Did you want me to give you something I don't believe in myself?' Everybody wants certainty, everybody wants security.

But what my experience tells me is that the basic religious instinct is a deep curiosity about why we are here. To find some existential truths to live by is, to my mind, so much better than putting on ready-made faith. There is a kind of exile implied in it, I know, but to me it's the more courageous path. As Rilke said, 'Learn to love the questions.' "

And of course, ready or not, the questions will come. For parents contemplating the choices before them, they are but the beginning.

Children and Religion

Chapter 1

BIG
QUESTIONS

"Eastertime is the worst for me, because it
meant so much to me once. Now
Easter morning comes, Emily gets her basket,
and that's it. But she asks what does Easter
mean and I don't know where to begin. I don't
know what I want her to know."

—Sarah Lang

Ten years ago, when our daughter was born, neither her father nor I gave much thought to what her religious future might be. Amid private speculations as to whether she would, in time, favor his family or mine, would turn to the cello or the piano, we managed only to discuss whether or not she would be baptized, then let the matter drop unresolved.

Both of us had been baptized in infancy—I into a Roman Catholic family that eventually numbered eight children, two of whom became nuns; he into an Episcopalian family that claimed a hymn-writing bishop in the last century, but whose own childhood religious experience peaked with compulsory chapel at boarding school.

As adults, we remained more than usually interested in religion—inveterate clippers of newspaper articles on the subject, possessors of multiple copies of the Old and New Testaments as well as James's *The Varieties of Religious Experience,* confident critics of both mainstream and fundamentalist theology. Yet we would most honestly have had to describe ourselves as nonbelievers—his nonbelief shakier than my own, perhaps—but both of us willing to thread our way through what an agnostic friend calls "the enigmas" by means of such substitute guides as literature, history, psychoanalytic theory, anthropology, and the inclinations of our own souls. Whether there was a God, and what one then ought to do about it, were irresistible and essential questions certainly, but they did not seem to require immediate answers. We could stand the existential heat, and the cold as well.

Whether Anna could fairly be expected to do the same was a question we managed to avoid asking ourselves, until her own spontaneous inquiries began landing about us like metaphysical shrapnel. As is true for many children, her earliest questions about the purpose of life and the existence of a hereafter centered on the death of someone she loved, in this case her eighty-two-year-old grandmother, who died as Anna was about to turn three.

"Why did Nanny die?" was her first, and not unexpected, question. "Because she was old and very sick, and because all people die eventually" was our first answer. "Why did Nanny die?" she returned immediately, and it took several more such questions and answers before we understood that it was not simple clarification she was after but a more rewarding explanation. From that moment on, she took to plumbing the existential depths regularly, forcing her parents both to reexamine their own beliefs and to consider, between improvisations, the potential effects of those beliefs on her.

"What does *dead* mean?" "How old is the world?" "Where do people go when they die?" These are, of course, all questions that can be dealt with on the material level, but as I waffled through an explanation of how her grandmother so quickly came to be reduced to boxable ash—who in his right mind would attempt to explain cremation to a three-year-old?—it became clear that we were not going to make it far on mechanistic explanations alone.

Nor, we soon realized, would her father and I long remain her exclusive informants. Within a few months, her friend Ian's grandmother had also died, but unlike Nanny, this lucky woman, according to her grandson, had gone straight to heaven, which turned out to be right where I had left it as a child, and where Anna—hearing about it, as far as we knew, for the first time—seemed to think it properly belonged: directly overhead, out of sight behind the clouds.

By this time she was in full pursuit of God, piecing him together from the conversations of friends and baby-sitters, from nursery school explanations of the various Jewish and Christian holidays, from greeting-card images, museum reproductions, and what suddenly seemed to be a ubiquitous social reference. Mentions of God and of church increased geometrically, with "Who is Jesus, is he God?" emerging as the next urgent question. "Some people think he was God," I answered easily enough. "Other people think he was just a good man." "I'm one of the people who thinks he was God," she told me one day as we were parking the car. She was not yet four. Some months later, having repeatedly drawn the same circumspect reply to the question, she prodded me further. "What do *you* believe?" she asked. "That he was a good man," I told her.

"That's what I think, too," she said.

Greater subtleties followed in time. "What religion are

we?" "Are Catholics the ones who think Jesus is God, or is it Jews who think that?" And one day as we were crossing the street, after weeks of Grimm's Fairy Tales, Halloween, and endless discussion of things "real" and "imaginary"—"God isn't in the real world, is he?"

In a matter of months, she had gone from apparently total innocence of metaphysical constructs to a preoccupation with the unseen and unknowable that landed her, and us, in the middle of territory we had somehow imagined ourselves circumnavigating—a territory claimed, disputed, partitioned, and jealously guarded for millennia by the various and competing forces of organized religion. Her every question, and our every hastily conceived answer, seemed suddenly to be freighted with consequences we could not possibly predict. How we responded to each isolated question might be of relatively little significance. Indeed, given her doggedness about most of these issues, there was always a second—or a third or a fourth—chance to come at a question. Cumulatively, however, it was clear that our answers were going to shape her worldview as surely as our parents' answers had shaped ours.

If in retrospect the process sounds inevitable, at the time it felt like a series of small electric shocks, each one as much of a surprise as the one that came before. Intending not to proselytize, we found ourselves prisoners of our own consistency and of a small child's logic and sometimes exhausting curiosity. You never really understand how handy the story of Adam and Eve is until, barely grasping the matter yourself, you've explained evolution to a four-year-old and been rewarded with "But how did the first person get born?" Nor is it possible to fully appreciate what a social lubricant the assumption of a shared piety is until you've tried to climb back out of the hole you've dug for yourself by broad-mindedly announcing, "No, we don't believe in God, but lots of other people do." "Why *do* they?" was her initial follow-up, later to alternate with the equally blunt, but surely more pertinent, "Why don't you?"

It is the certain fate of every parent to be obliged at some point to deal with, or duck, similar questions, either alone or from the shelter of the faith he or she professes.

"The kids were the impetus for us," said Sue Gilger of her decision to join a local church after many years of noninvolvement. "All the things they were asking about were like second nature to me. I knew all the stories, they were in my head, but I didn't have the ability to teach them what I wanted them to know."

"The moment you have a child, you begin to think about these issues in a new way," said one father who was raising his child within the Protestant tradition despite deep uncertainty about the divinity of Christ and other matters of faith. "But I don't think it's only because of embarrassing questions. It's more a question of 'Should this child know what's in the Bible because of the philosophy it espouses, and of how that will enrich her understanding of life?' "

What might have been a relatively simple matter for previous generations, bound together by common beliefs and traditions and largely isolated from contrary points of view, has come to be an immensely complicated matter for many parents today. "Religious education has become thornier than sex education," observes Anna Quindlen, a columnist for the *New York Times* whose writing reflects a parent's struggle to teach her children moral values and compassion as well as a certain impatience, as a practicing Catholic, with the official viewpoint. "When we were kids, our parents sent us to Catholic school, and there was the Baltimore Catechism—bingo, end of discussion. Having to handle it yourself would have been difficult enough for my parents. It's more difficult for someone like me who has to equivocate."

In a sense we know too much—and too little. On the one hand, we have credible explanations for much of the natural phenomena that once baffled humankind, as well as reason to believe that the remaining mysteries of physical life will in time be revealed. On the other, we are no closer to knowing why we are here or where we are going than our most ancient ancestors, who at least had the comfort of imagining themselves at the cozy center of a modest and newly minted universe.

Thus while the old metaphysical certainties have been undermined—some would say obliterated—no new ones have taken their place. "I don't know what I want her to know," is how Sarah Lang put it finally, and she might have been speaking for the majority of parents with whom I have talked over the last several years. It is not just a matter of one's private indecisiveness but a recognition that the choices one makes in answering a child's questions inevitably lead somewhere, opening up certain paths, foreclosing others. Struggling to answer their children's earliest and grandest big questions—how old is the world, where did God come from, will the world ever end—parents instinctively know they are rehearsing for the stickier, more intimate philosophical questions to come—how do people know there is a heaven if nobody has seen it, why are some people poor and some people rich, why do children get diseases, why do planes crash, why is it against the law to kill yourself, why are people always arguing about abortion? One has only to watch the evening news with a child to discover how uncertainly one's own equilibrium is maintained by one's private beliefs—instinctive or acquired, and frequently contradictory—about the origins and workings of man and nature.

The majority of the *Why?*s with which my daughter interrupts Peter Jennings's nightly bulletins, for instance, tend to require explanations that combine several hundred years' worth of history, political treachery, religious antagonism, plus the occasional scientific or economic theory, which I am equally incompetent to explain. Even more consistently, however, they require something less factual and more radical by way of an answer, a response that simultaneously addresses the fundamental riddle of earthly injustice and eternal redress, of the child's instinctive awareness of the possibility of "something more" and the simple human desire to be reassured.

Given the conspicuous shortage of reassuring answers, then, what sense does it make to dispense with the familiar, if imperfect, answers supplied by religion? Doesn't the parent owe the child security first of all, and shouldn't all answers to existential questions therefore be comforting—namely, that there is life after death, that God is watching out for you, that there is order in the universe, and that justice will ultimately prevail?

Theology aside, one could legitimately argue that the symbols and conventions of religion offer children a vision of security rivaled only by the family itself, and ultimately surpassing it. The problem is that for many

people neither the symbols nor the conventions offer lasting comfort; nor do they come without strings attached.
The cost of making use of them, therefore, has somehow
to be measured against one's past and present convictions,
or confusion. "It is still easier to sit in a pew for an hour
a week than to contemplate these questions alone," said
Larry Small, who was raised in a strict Baptist family in
the Midwest but whose children are being raised without
any religion. "When you give up religion, it's a little
scary."

But it is not only the "unchurched" who must sort out
what it is they mean to have their children believe—which
is why there is an audience for talks like one I attended
at an Episcopal church to which some good friends belong. The young woman priest leading the discussion,
who happened to be a former Roman Catholic, opened
the session by reciting some of the questions children
typically ask about God and religion, what I would term
a mixture of "big" and secondary questions. "What does
God look like?" "Is it really Jesus' blood?" "Why do we
have to go to church?"

The priest did not then proceed to fill in the blanks but
rather to acknowledge that "there are no simple answers,"
something her audience had already discovered at home,
though they might be forgiven for hoping to find some
at this forum. What followed instead was an intelligent
and sympathetic talk that covered a considerable amount
of ground, from the meaning of faith—defined as a "disposition of the heart" rather than "a body of knowledge
we can transfer to children, like Greek"—and its refinement and deepening in stages over a lifetime, to the importance of community, the usefulness of the Bible

("something we tend to overlook because of all this fundamentalist stuff"), and the value of ritual as "the symbolic expression of our deepest desires."

"The question is not how can we make our children Christians?" the priest said, "but how can we be Christians together?" When it was time for questions, however, literalism immediately reared its head once more.

"My son asked me," said one father, "whether, if God was here on Sundays, was he in other churches as well?"

"I have a three-and-a-half-year-old who wanted to know what angels look like," said another.

A third parent recounted her confusion when her two-and-a-half-year-old announced that "Jesus must be in the clouds." She thought somehow that she should correct that image but didn't know where to start.

The priest responded by recalling how when she first enrolled in the seminary her young sons asked her why she wanted to become a priest, and she found herself caught up short. "What we believe is so private," she said, that it is difficult to put into words. "God is almost a bigger taboo than sex. How much do I say, in what tone of voice? It demands an intimacy with yourself."

Trying to address a few of the specific questions, she then suggested to the father whose child wanted to know what angels look like, "You could say a lot of people have different ideas of what they might look like. Show them some different artists' interpretations and ask them what they think angels might look like." Seeing how this small group of well-educated and earnest parents were hanging on her every tentative word, she suddenly laughed and said, "You're worried that heaven's not going to turn out like you told them, aren't you?"

It is, indeed, for many in this generation, as if we fear being found out—found foolish, found naïve, found wrong. We are plagued by the idea that, as with all other things, there is a right way to do this; that just as it is possible, with the right sort of information, to protect against dental plaque and arterial plaque, against birth defects, nuclear war, and being taken for a ride when buying a new car, there exists a way not to repeat the mistakes of our parents, a way to avert both religious resentment and spiritual ennui, to give children what they need but not what will trap or limit them.

The difficulty is in discovering how. In *A Good Enough Parent,* Bruno Bettelheim talks of the unprecedented dilemma of the modern parent seeking to do the right thing. "Books telling parents how they ought to raise their children are not exactly a new phenomenon," he writes. "But only in this century, and particularly since the 1950s, have they been so popular, with large numbers of parents turning to them for advice and comfort when feeling uncertain about how to handle the problems they encounter in raising their children. With the disintegration of traditional modes of family life and of the rearing of children, in the wake of our century's massive urbanization and industrialization, we have lost the security people once derived from long-standing customs, from growing up as part of a large, extended family and from all other experiences these provided."

Parents suffering from precisely that sense of cultural dislocation are among those who sign up for the parenting courses conducted by developmental psychologists Lisa Spiegel and Jean Kunhardt in lower Manhattan.

"We talk about a lot of things in our parenting groups,

from sleep problems to infant sexuality," says Kunhardt. "Religion is just one of them, but while it is not an issue for everyone, for some, and especially those who are partners in a mixed marriage, it is an important 'underground' issue—something that has not been discussed but is causing problems. We don't push any particular resolution, but we use it as a spark to get parents talking about what they might want to do. Because it is such a hard thing for some people to deal with," says Kunhardt, who is herself a partner in a Jewish-Christian marriage, "many simply throw out the baby with the bathwater and do nothing. And they end up losing out on some things they might really benefit from as a family."

Not surprisingly, such parents frequently feel they are reinventing the wheel. "There is a lot of stress with respect to the idea that there is a perfect way to do things," says Spiegel. "It is almost as if parents feel they must make choices, either-or, that they are not prepared to make. It is very hard for them to see that they can occupy a middle ground. Some, of course, identify with their own parents and therefore attempt to make their decisions similarly, but a lot of new parents are trying to repair things from their own childhoods, and they often think they have to do things differently. It has to do with a sense of legitimacy," suggests Spiegel, "as well as a determination never to make the mistakes their parents made. Yet there is still a need to refer to some authority, some expert out there somewhere. A generation ago it was the mother, the grandmother. Today it's the book, or the parenting group."

In fact, Spiegel and Kunhardt are somewhat unusual in their attention to the subject. For while the uncertain modern parent can find plenty of substitute counsel on infant sleep patterns, toilet training, and the native anti-social behavior of two-year-olds, comparable wisdom is generally wanting on the interrelated subjects of God, religious upbringing, and the psychological value of a belief in the hereafter. There is no listing in the index of Benjamin Spock's *Baby and Child Care* capable of reas-suring the generation commonly thought to have been raised on his views: no reference to "religion," to "God," or to "Sunday school," and certainly no hint of the role religion has traditionally played in shaping the child's worldview. (In his more discursive *Dr. Spock on Parenting*, the pediatrician does include a brief section titled "God and Religion in the Agnostic Family," sandwiched be-tween discussions of pets and fairy tales.) Nor is there anything in any of Berry Brazelton's work or in Penelope Leach's *Your Baby and Child*—nothing that remarks the subject as significant or troublesome, nothing that ac-knowledges its cultural ubiquity or its curious contradic-tory role, at once peripheral and ineluctable, in modern life.

The pattern continues through Leach's more expansive work, *Your Growing Child, Babyhood Through Adolescence*, Selma Fraiberg's popular *The Magic Years*, Dr. Haim Gin-ott's *Between Parent and Child*, Theresa and Frank Caplan's *The Early Childhood Years*. To find an extended discussion of the subject, one must turn, as Sarah Lang did when her older daughter became obsessed with religion at about the age of five, to *Infant and Culture*, the classic work by Arnold Gesell and Frances L. Ilg, first published in 1943.

By contrast to the perspective of most other experts, the authors of *Infant and Culture* plainly acknowledge consciousness of God to be part of the child's natural development. But to any parent who might be struggling with disbelief, or whose skepticism about formal religion is what sent him in search of advice in the first place, Gesell and Ilg's presentation offers small comfort. For that matter, Gesell and Ilg offer little to any parent who falls outside the Christian majority. In a section titled "Cultural and Creative Activities," the interest of a four-year-old in a range of religious holidays and practices is summarized in this way:

2. Christmas. There is a real interest in the story of Jesus, which is talked about and dramatized . . . the child asks for specific toys. . . .

4. Easter. Still believes in the Easter Bunny . . . still no conception of the meaning of Easter. . . .

7. Religion. May sit through a small part of the service, epecially the music, but should not be expected to sit through the entire service. . . . Marked interest in death, heaven, etc. Begins questioning as to the source of things: who made the sun, moon, world.

The common answer, "God," either settles the topic without his finding out what he wanted to know, or may lead to the asking of ludicrous questions about God.

In Gesell's *The Child from Five to Ten,* still in print after forty-four years, and more likely than *Infant and Culture* to be found on a bookshelf at home, this vision of a homogeneous Christian universe remains undisturbed: "The age of six is often the peak period in these middle years of the child's interest in a creative power to which he can relate himself. . . . He grasps the concept of God as the creator of the world, of animals and of beautiful things. . . . Six asks to go to Sunday School . . . could hear the story of the little Lord Jesus over and over again. . . . Prayers become important to him. He feels confident that his prayers will be answered. If his mother would pray for a boy, he feels confident that she would receive one. . . ."

No doubt Gesell was correct in his developmental observations of middle-class children raised in the 1940s, and no doubt many of those observations remain accurate. The "six" who "could hear the story of the little Lord Jesus over and over again" would have as much company in his delight today as then, the story of the Christ Child having no rival as an affirmation of human worth and, most particularly, of the value of a baby to its immediate family and to the larger world.

Similarly, while many fewer "sixes" attend Sunday school today than when Gesell did his research, many a "six" still asks to go, especially if his best friend does. (When my daughter first slipped into one of the crimson robes worn by the children at her friend Elizabeth's Episcopal church, she, like their mutual friend Kate a few weeks earlier, was ready to sign up for life. She has since been swayed by the "kids' club" at the Unitarian church of another friend, and I suspect she would forswear all other rites if she could be married off like the eldest daughter in *Fiddler on the Roof,* with a candlelight procession of neighbors through the village.) At the same time, to judge from the dozen or so Sunday school classes I've observed, there are a lot of children who would rather be skateboarding, sleeping, or playing Nintendo than connecting dots to make a picture of an angel, or stumbling through a parable while being kicked under the table by an even more reluctant pupil—a natural enough split among children and one that is replicated when it comes to individual curiosity as to "the source of things."

For every incessant questioner who interrupts adult conversation to ask whether the sun came first, or God, or the dinosaurs, there is, by parental accounting, another who passes through childhood in a state of profound metaphysical disinterest—an attitude summed up by the mother of one such boy as, "Mom, some people think too much."

Children's instincts for explanation and order, for parental idealization, for cultural as well as familial confirmation of the importance of the birth of a child have not changed much. What has changed—and the reason one turns from Gesell in frustration—is that for so many parents, the context and the accompanying assumptions that once insured religious continuity have dissolved, rendering Gesell's once-comforting observations as meaningful as a Victorian treatise on household management.

The inattention of most popular texts to the subject, on the other hand, demonstrates the degree to which religious belief and practice have become dissociated from everyday concerns and from the larger culture. That conventional psychology and developmental theory might have no opinion *whatsoever* on the significance of religious training to children's well-being began to seem possible after I contacted one of the country's most distinguished and best-known authorities on childhood development. "It's a very good question you've got there," he said, then added, with stunning, if admirable, candor, "I have to say I've never given it any thought, really."

In fact, depending on whom you consult, you might well conclude that formal religion has become entirely peripheral to children's interior lives (and to their parents' as well) at the same time as you decide that the principal concerns of children and religion are interchangeable. Thus I was credibly informed by several of the child psychologists to whom I addressed the question that the subject of religion simply never came up, while an equal number spoke of it as a powerful and consistent factor in children's psychological adaptations. Ultimately, I suspect, the discrepancy may have more to do with the expectations and confessed biases of the therapists than with what is going on in children's minds, or how important formal religion is to the larger family.

Barbara Fields, a New York therapist whose personal perspective is agnostic, detects little overtly religious material in her work with children and their families. "All the kids I treat are very involved in questions of birth and death, for example, but I've never heard a parent explain either in religious terms. It's as if there are two separate streams, what they talk about at home and what is talked about at church or in synagogue."

Similarly, says Fields, the familiar stories and traditions of her young patients' official religions very rarely come into play in therapy, suggesting that their psychological influence is not terribly strong. On the other hand, she says, remarking on a phenomenon familiar to any parent who has watched his child at play, "children are very mythic. They think very primitively and are continually making things up in order to make sense of the world."

While essentially in agreement that children think in mythic and animistic terms, pediatric psychiatrist Dr. Sirgay Sanger is more explicit in identifying that instinct as religious in nature. "Children *invent* religion in order to explain the world," says Sanger, "in order to explain sickness or loss, to explain why they don't have four grandparents or why a mother's pregnancy did not result in a brother or a sister. Left to themselves, children come up with explanations that mimic every religion in the world—Christian, Buddhist, Jewish, Hindu, Muslim. They construct all sort of explanations to satisfy them- selves—ladders going straight up to heaven, tree spirits, misbehavior causing family disaster."

Dr. Harvey Roy Greenberg, a professor of psychiatry at Albert Einstein Medical School in New York, and a Buddhist, takes a similar view. Given the universal human need to look for answers, or, at any rate, to pose the significant questions, says Greenberg, "You could say that everybody has an innate religiosity. The first indi- cation of this in children comes when they start to look at where things end, at about age three to four, and when they start to ask, 'Who made me?' My bias is to call them religious questions, but let's just say they are existential questions.

"It makes an enormous difference to children in how parents treat those questions. Our parents are all that stand between us and existential uncertainty. It can be anxious- making for little kids to hear their parents waffling on these questions. It's better to stand for something than to waffle. On the other hand, if the parent is seriously waf- fling on these issues and is willing to discuss his confusion with the kid, that's okay. The worst thing for adolescents, who take these matters very seriously, is to have their questions fobbed off by their parents. 'Go ask the min- ister,' or 'What are you worrying about that for?'

"With little kids, you have to answer these questions

simply and firmly, but you have to find out what their real worries are. While for adolescents the issue is usually existential, for little children, the issue is often one of anxiety.''

As both Greenberg and Sanger point out, small children are far more concerned with immediate events and a feeling of security than they are with any protracted metaphysical speculations. When a child who has lost one parent asks the surviving parent if *he* is going to die, for instance, the last thing she wants to hear is, well, we all die. She's not interested in your inevitable demise at seventy-five or eighty-three. She wants to be told that you are not going to die next week, before her next birthday, or before you've finished the Christmas shopping.

It is in recognition of this immediacy of interest, then, that parents can best respond to children's questions about life and death. The inevitable next issue for parents is how to integrate the child's true needs with the religious beliefs one hopes to pass on to them.

"When Lisa was about three, she became obsessed with death. Nobody she knew had died, but she was always asking me, 'Why do people die, where do they go when they die?' One day, we were crossing Broadway, hand in hand, and there in the middle of the traffic island was a dead pigeon. I was terrified. Here was this dead thing right in our path. What was I going to say? And then Lisa said, perfectly cheerfully, 'Oh, look, a dead pigeon!' And I thought, 'Yes, Lisa, and someday we will be dead pigeons, too.' "

—Nancy Gallin

Apart from the existence and nature of God, there is, of course no bigger "big" question than what happens to us after death—and no surer guarantee that the subject of religion will be introduced into the family, ready or not. So it is instructive to contrast the general lack of interest in religion displayed by the authors of child-rearing guides with the considerable attention that virtually all of them devote to children's concerns about death.

Penelope Leach spends no fewer than eleven pages on the subject, Selma Fraiberg eight, Haim Ginott five, Benjain Spock four. Yet except for the most perfunctory sort of acknowledgement that a parent's attitude toward the afterlife might bear on his handling of questions about death, all approach the subject from a resolutely secular perspective, seeking variously to reassure children that disaster will not befall them personally (or that if it does, it will soon be set right), and to help them distinguish between fantasy and reality while insuring that parents allow their children to feel and to mourn.

However varied their respective treatments, cumulatively it is as if there were no immaterial component to the subject, no confusion about how to reconcile the certainty of death and the longing for immortality, no history of man attempting to make sense of life through just this issue. The separation of church and couch is complete, belying the muddle ordinary parents find themselves in on the question.

In *The Magic Years,* for example, as part of a section titled "The Right to Feel," Selma Fraiberg relates a friend's worries about how to break the news of a pet hamster's death to her five-year-old son. The friend confesses that she cannot bear to deliver the truth without a palliative. "I thought I would tell him that Ernest (the hamster) went to heaven. Would it be all right to tell him that?"

"Only if you're sure that Ernest went to heaven," Fraiberg teases. Then the friend asks, "How can he possibly know what death means?" To which Fraiberg gives the thoroughly down-to-earth answer: "But isn't this how he will know what death means? Do we ever know more about death than this—the reaction to the loss of someone loved?"

The religious option is more tenderly treated by both Spock and Ginott, though it is interesting to note how differently they interpret the psychological effect of heaven. Locating his discussion of death under the category of children's fears, Spock frames his advice accordingly. "All healthy people of every age," he writes, "have some degree of fear and resentment of death. There is no way to present this matter to children that will get around this basic human attitude. But if you think of death as something to be met with dignity and fortitude, you'll be able to give somewhat the same feeling about it to your child."

Ginott, too, begins with hard realism. "To adults," he writes, "the tragedy of death lies in its irreversibility. Death, so final and eternal, is the end of all hope." A bit later he beats a retreat to a more optimistic outlook. "The consolation that faith brings," he writes, "[is that] it offers man a future, so he may live and die in peace." Spock similarly veers from his sober secular counsel to include a religious variation, though one suspects it is a formulation he cannot have thought through very carefully. "Some parents like to express it in religious terms: 'He was very, very sick and God took him to Heaven to take care of him.' Remember to hug her and smile at her and remind her that you're going to be together for years and years."

Unless, of course—was my immediate reaction—one of you gets very, very sick, and God decides to take you to heaven to take care of you! (I heard an even more alarmist view of heaven from a woman whose husband died when her daughter was three. She insisted that no one mention heaven to her daughter, because she said, the belief that one's longed-for parent was in heaven was "a sure prescription for teenage suicide.") In a similar vein, Ginott concludes his discussion of the subject of an afterlife with the unanticipated response of a five-year-old patient. Told that his grandmother had "gone to heaven and become an angel," the child began to pray that the rest of the family would die and become angels too.

No such confusion is likely to result from consulting Penelope Leach, whose extended discussion of the subject in *Your Growing Child* begins with an observation that underscores parental ambivalence about the meaning of death and its significance to children, even as it overlooks the underlying cause of that ambivalence. "Few children today," she writes, "are brought up in ignorance of what we call 'the facts of life,' but most are still kept in ignorance of the other end of that life cycle: death. . . . Young children cannot anticipate tragedy and grief nor empathize with people who are thus suffering. They are therefore curious about death in exactly the same way that they are curious about other aspects of life, until they find that their parents cannot answer their questions straightforwardly: that death is still the Great Unmentionable."

In laying the groundwork for the practical advice to follow, Leach presents what amounts to a philosophical discourse on death as a natural phenomenon. Among the boldface subheads that introduce discussions meant to help parents acquaint children with death's reality and its naturalness are: "Everything That Lives, Dies"; "Different Living Things Live on Different Time Scales"; "That Death Is Necessary for Renewal"; and "That New, Young Creatures Are Needed Because Old Ones Wear Out." Significantly, it is a reality that begins and ends with biology, a nature defined by the cycle of physical renewal and replacement. And, except for a brief aside, it exludes the metaphysical aspect altogether.

"Whatever you wish to teach your child about a possible life after death," she writes in polite dismissal, "it is vital that every child understand that bodies (of whatever creature) never *ever* come back to life and never *ever* have any consciousness, any feeling, any life remaining. . . . It is important to work at this one while the matter can be impersonal, because when a child does face a death which matters to her, the feelings of the corpse and the horrors of its disposal are usually a main source of anxiety."

Both the philosophical underpinnings of Leach's approach and the detailed practical advice that follow have a humane and convincing tone. Her treatment is nonetheless remarkable for its failure to acknowledge the central role religion has traditionally played in dealing with the human fear of death. "Religion is the human response to the dual reality of being alive and knowing we have

to die," says Forrester Church, a Unitarian minister who
has written extensively on faith and its origins in human
needs. "We are the only creatures who *know* we are going
to die."

Over and over, parents who neither believed in an afterlife nor voluntarily offered it to their children as solace
reported their reluctance to deprive their children of a
concept of heaven acquired elsewhere once it became clear
how comforting they found it. Penny Coleman, for instance, has attended to her children's fears about death
since their earliest expression and has addressed their
greatest fear—that something would happen to both her
and their father—by reassuring them that many people
love them and would take care of them in the extremely
unlikely event that something happened. Heaven was not
part of her carefully framed assurances, so she was surprised by her son Charlie's reaction to the death of a
classmate when he was about three. "All the Catholic
kids came to school totally serene, saying, 'He's in heaven
with the angels.' And Charlie, who has heard something
of heaven and hell from one of his cousins, came home
from school, looked me in the eye as if to say, I dare you,
and announced, 'I believe in heaven, Mom.' I didn't want
to take it away from him."

Dan Menaker sensed a comparable need in his young
son when the parent of a classmate died. "It's a fine moral
question," Menaker, an atheist, observed, "to deprive
children of the right or the ability to believe in heaven,
which is a valid human concept. To do so may be as great
a transgression as lying about what you believe. So when
Willy tells me that the parent of this classmate died and
that he is in heaven, I don't say, 'Yes, he's in heaven,' or

'No, he's not.' I let it go and assume that we will talk
about it again when he's older.''

To some extent, of course, heaven is in the public do-
main, an all-purpose convention and comfort that, like
hell, is available to parents of every persuasion.

"When my father became ill recently," Lisa Spiegel
recalled, "my daughter became obsessed by death. She
kept asking me, 'Where do people go after they die?' and
all my non-answers were too upsetting for her. She
needed something to hold on to, and in sheer desperation
I found myself bringing in heaven. And even as I did it,
I was thinking, '*Oh,* that's how they invented heaven.' ''

Employed by a parent for whom it has no personal
religious significance, the idea of heaven as simply a
peaceful, pain-free address after life as we know it is not
unlike opening the closet door wide so a child can make
sure there are no monsters lurking behind the clothes.
Thus when a sweet seven-year-old boy in my daughter's
second-grade class died at the end of an illness that lasted
three months, the parents of most of the kids—regardless
of their private convictions or lack of formal religious
connection—chose to comfort their children by telling
them that Zachie had indeed gone to heaven. More surprising, and infinitely more poignant to me, was the regret expressed by Zachie's mother, an atheist and
heretofore resolutely antireligious woman who had with-
stood the ruinous siege with heroic composure, that she
had not conjured heaven for her son's comfort before he
died. "I think he would have been less scared," she said.

Someone brought up with a traditional belief in heaven,
on the other hand, is likely to come at the subject rather
differently. Jenny Allen, who grew up as an Episcopalian

and is distantly related to the family of a famous American preacher, might best be described these days, with deliberate redundancy, as an uncertain agnostic. Her husband, the cartoonist Jules Feiffer, is an unconfused (though bar mitzvahed) atheist, and they have a young daughter, Halley, whose first experience of death, when Jules' sister died a few years ago, caught Jenny off balance.

"Jules and I were talking about what to tell Halley, and fooling around, he said in this joking way, 'Well, we could tell her she died and went to heaven'—almost as if we could actually do this. And the weird thing is that it never had occurred to me—I who grew up on the idea of heaven, I who am always trying to protect her from things. Why didn't it occur to me? In part, it was because of Jules, I suppose, and in part because of his sister, who would have been horrified at the idea, but more because of myself. I couldn't get the words out. To have said, 'She died and went to heaven'—it would have been so loaded a commitment. I would have been saying, 'This is what I believe, and I want you to share these beliefs.' It was such a powerful image that I had to know whether I believed it before I imparted it to her. The subject makes me uneasy because I haven't resolved it."

Implicit in such uneasiness is the idea that there *is* some tidy resolution to be reached, and that if one were the sort of right-thinking person entitled to raise a child, one would reach it. Heaven does or doesn't exist, period. No off-loading of adult ambivalence on innocent children. They need to know there will be dinner on the table tonight and a hereafter in the hereafter. Or do they?

As the center of their own worlds, very young children tend to interpret events exclusively in terms of how they will be affected. "When a pet is being trained, for example," says Sanger, "children find it logical to expect the same harsh treatment for themselves. And when a parent or grandparent dies, a pre-schooler's subjectivity leads him to feel responsible. Children's need for explanation is much greater than adults', who have science, biology, and the ways of the world to cushion events. Children have to run as fast as they can in their minds to create coherence in a confusing world. Though some of their conclusions alarm adults—thinking they are responsible for a relative's death, for instance—to their way of thinking, at least some sense has been injected into a situation that otherwise would be painfully mystifying. The child's imaginative explanation spares him the sense of being adrift in an unsafe world."

In other words, just like adults, they make up things they cannot possibly know in order to comfort themselves, or to give shape to their inchoate fears. Like adults, too, some of their inventions will be more successful than others—more rewarding, more comforting. Some will be pretty terrifying. Surely no adult in my childhood meant heaven to be as agonizing a prospect as my busy little brain made it, or as many people I've talked to found it—a place so bland and blindingly blissful that I was almost as worried about spending eternity there as I was about spending it in hell. (What troubled me most, though, was the problem of *eternity*. An *hour* is an eternity to a child. What is one to make of a time frame painstakingly compared to the emptying of oceans by thimbles-full?)

In his hugely successful evangelical crusades in the 1950s, Billy Graham, calculating from biblical references, used to descry a heaven "1,600 miles wide, 1,600 miles long, and 1,600 miles high," but no adult I've talked to lately would care to so much as point a finger in a likely direction, and many of the clergy would just as soon avoid stratospheric precision as well.

"I would never tell a child that someone who died was in heaven," said one woman I talked to, citing the advice of her minister. "I would say that God is taking care of them. The important thing is for them to know that God *will* take care of them and that death is therefore nothing to be afraid of."

Even among Catholics, who once employed a complicated cartography of the hereafter that included not just heaven and hell but limbo and purgatory as well, "we try," one young parish priest told me, "not to push a particular cloud." To believers and former believers alike, heaven is not the North Pole but a metaphysical lode star, not a geographical terminus but a state of grace, not a location but a different form of existence.

The heaven my sister Ginny described as we sat talking with our children one day, is neither place nor reward but a state of final understanding and union with God, the end to the riddle, the logical punctuation to faith. "To me, heaven is your relationship with God," she said, then interrupted herself with a short laugh to make clear that she was speaking out of personal conviction, not certainty. "Of course, I don't *know*," she said. "It's just my perception. But I do think there's an afterlife, some survival of the soul."

Jenny Allen's intuitive certainty that there was something major at stake if she gave her daughter heaven had to do not with being obliged to pass on Billy Graham's heaven, or some wild apocalyptic vision, but with her incapacity to get behind even so benign a conviction as my sister's. To offer a child heaven is to imply something significant, and one had better be prepared for its consequences. With heaven one introduces not just a different scale of fantasy but a different conception of reality altogether, one that includes the existence of a parallel universe that is real but unseen, and implicitly superior or more fulfilling than the one the child knows for himself. If one does not believe in that universe, what is the point of advertising its real estate?

Like Jenny Allen, I could not possibly have gotten the word *heaven* out of my mouth for my daughter's benefit the first time death came up—nor have I since—yet even as I groped for words to express what I did believe, it was as if some earlier self was watching in astonishment: Are you seriously going to tell the child that life *ends* at death? How could you?

The stakes, once I had reviewed them, were of course more powerfully psychological than theological, and in worrying so earnestly over the second I had not attended much to the first, until the question took me by the throat. Coming from an entirely different direction, I had arrived, like Lisa Spiegel, at the perfectly surprising moment of recognition—so that's why they invented heaven! But in contrast to her uncomplicated and presumably temporary borrowing of the idea, my previously complete credulousness on the subject barred me from employing it. Despite its enormous psychological appeal, the fact that it had once been credible and now seemed purely fantastic made it impossible for me to pass it on to Anna. And like answering her first questions about sex, the easiest thing turned out to be to tell the truth as

I understood it: I don't know what happens to us after death, and I don't think anyone else does either. But whatever it is, it has happened to millions of people before us. It is what happens to humans. It is what happens to all life.

Similarly, Candace Burnett talked of how she would like her children "to grow up believing they're going to live forever, but if I lied to them, they'd smell it." What she offers them instead is the view she inclines toward personally, which has no more basis in her Congregationalist upbringing than mine does in a Catholic past— a sense of the soul's continuance she describes as being "more like reincarnation than heaven and hell." To judge from a survey conducted for *Newsweek* in 1989, she is not alone. It turns out that a quarter of all Americans believe in reincarnation, as compared to three-quarters who still believe in heaven (with three-quarters of the latter group expecting to actually get there).

Once one lets go the heavenly vista, of course, the really appealing alternatives narrow rather abruptly. Why not reincarnation, then? Uncluttered by Eastern peculiarities, this nonspecific hedge against oblivion is cheerfully perceived as being not at all incompatible with Western, or Judeo-Christian, theology, only one more entree in the smorgasbord to which we are automatically entitled in the global religious restaurant. For a generation unfettered by theology and more certain than ever that one person's guess is as good as another's, the choice between heaven and spiritual recycling is both as arbitrary and legitimate as any other religious choice, a reflection of one's personal disposition more than of any powerfully held conviction. Clearly, there remain millions of believers for whom the idea of heaven is an absolute article of personal faith as well as the accepted answer given by their particular creed. Yet if one looks at the subject of an afterlife not as some carrot-and-stick proposition linked to good behavior but primarily in terms of the obligation to reassure, then in fact what one is after is simply the answer one is personally most comfortable passing along.

As one Protestant mother sensibly observed, "It is easy to understand why someone who doesn't believe in heaven would want to offer their children reincarnation. Because we *have* heaven, and have no trouble with the idea, we don't happen to need an alternative. But I can see why other people might."

A few months after my daughter and her friend Ian had first discussed the fates of their respective grandmothers, her father overheard them talking about it again while playing. Since their first exchange, we had wondered from time to time whether Anna might have felt cheated that Ian's grandmother had gone to heaven while hers was shut up in the front hall closet. But it seemed not to be the case.

"I miss my grandma," Ian said. "She's in heaven." "Where is heaven?" Anna asked. "It's up in the sky. It's a big planet. Bigger than Mars, with blue fire all around it." "Well," said Anna, "my grandmother's turned to dust already and we've got her in a box."

"From science, I know everything after Adam and Eve, but before science, that's what I wonder. How the trees got there? I believe God did it, but somehow it's kind of hard to explain."

—Jessica Zenk, aged ten

Though they tend to come up at a somewhat later point, questions about the origins of the world or the workings of nature can trigger a comparable moment of truth for parents—arrived at just as abruptly and demanding an equally fundamental confession of conviction, belief, doubt, or mystification.

A hundred years ago, a parent or a Sunday school teacher could confidently attribute all natural phenomena to the beneficent, if occasionally hard to discern, hand of God. Western cosmology was seamless, purposeful, and, for all practical purposes, universally subscribed to. "It was supposed and taught," writes Joseph Campbell in *Myths to Live By,* "that there had been, quite concretely, a creation of the world in seven days by a god known only to the Jews; that somewhere on this broad new earth there had been a Garden of Eden containing a serpent that could talk; that the first woman, Eve, was formed from the first man's rib, and that the wicked serpent told her of the marvelous properties of the fruits of a certain tree of which God had forbidden the couple to eat; and that as a consequence of their having eaten of that fruit, there followed a 'Fall' of all mankind, death came into the world, and the couple was driven forth from the garden. For there was in the center of that garden a second tree, the fruit of which would have given them eternal life; and their creator, fearing lest they should now take and eat of that, too, and so become as knowing and immortal as himself, cursed them, and having driven them out, placed at his garden gate 'cherubim and a flaming sword which turned every way to guard the way to the tree of life.' "

"It seems impossible today," Campbell continued

(writing in 1966), "but people actually believed all that until as recently as half a century or so ago: clergymen, philosophers, government officers and all."

A. N. Wilson repeats the point in his revisionist *Eminent Victorians,* observing that "the majority of educated people" through the close of the nineteenth century accepted the Bible not just as moral guide but as credible physical and biological reference.

The inference meant to be drawn from both writers is of course that no thinking person could believe such nonsense. Yet it seems equally obvious that the image of a fully conceived world brought into existence by a highly imaginative and loving Creator retains enormous emotional force today, somehow coexisting with a space-age cosmology to which few of us have yet adjusted. We are made woozy by a surfeit of incomprehensible numbers— of uncharted distances and light years in the billions, of species long extinct, of stars and galaxies beyond tallying—and with the accumulated evidence of what Stephen Jay Gould calls evolutionary "contingency," the idea that our very appearance in time is an accident of opportunity that might never have been.

It is a conception of life, and human significance, that, absent a meliorating mythology, seems to violate the adult ego as profoundly as death. Is that all we amount to, and if so, then what exactly is the point? Where is the need for *us,* where the overspilling of love that leads to human incarnation? Few of the people I talked to were willing to accede wholly to the notion that we are here because we are here, choosing rather to resolve the question of human centrality and purpose by means of revisionist religious tradition, personal logic, sheer insistence, or some combination thereof. When I asked Constance Beavon, for example, a friend who is a practicing Episcopalian, whether she would begin with Genesis or science in discussing the origin of the world with her daughters, her answer was unequivocal. "I would absolutely begin with the scientific explanation," she said, "but then I would go *on*." For her, the visible world abounds with evidence of a divine hand, while the biblical story of Creation appears a prescient metaphor for what science has demonstrated about the origins of the universe.

Similarly, when my sister Ginny's children ask her what she makes of evolution, she tells them, "It makes sense to me, even if it's not proven," and she is pleased by the fact that her two older children "both came to the conclusion, independently, that because of all the different races around the world, we couldn't come from the same parents or we'd all be alike."

At the same time, she says, "I don't have a problem telling them there are lots of things we don't understand, and that they don't have to worry about it. And while I don't think that God is sitting up there moving things around as if on a chessboard, I always tell them that I think God started nature. I'm not sure what the purpose of life is, but I do think there is one or there would be chaos."

The biblical calendar may be off by eons in this view, but Michelangelo's imagery of the divine spark remains fundamentally correct, its underlying truth untouched. It is a position in which the believing parent is understandably at home. "When I read fairy tales to my children," said John Winters, an Episcopalian with two young daughters, "I always make it clear that these are stories meant to explain things in life but that they are fiction. I would explain Bible stories the same way—that they too are fiction meant to explain things, but that they were written by people who felt very close to God."

The instinct to resolve the mystery in favor of meaning, however undefined, is not confined to traditional believers. "I am in absolute awe of the design of the universe," said Paul Fargis. "When I see that the mechanism is working, that my heart is pumping x number of gallons of blood through my system every second, then I think there must be some purpose behind it." "I'm much more comfortable with the idea of there being some kind of 'force' than anything else," said Wendy Kaufman. "It can be a man, or a woman, or some other image. It doesn't matter. But something as complex as your body—I firmly believe that it's more than some freak accident. Even for an accident to happen—there has to have been something to have an accident in."

For other parents, as for me personally, the challenge has been to come to terms with the apparent absence of a connection between our origins and the meaning we give to life. "I was working with Kate on an assignment one night about magnetism and the North and South poles," said Eileen Gillooly, "and she kept asking, 'But why does it work this way,' and I was struggling to explain about mineral deposits and why they are where they are, all in as scientific a manner as I could manage, but all the time I was thinking, '*I* don't know, that's just the way it *is*.' And I realized that I am comfortable with not knowing. I can say, yes, the accident of life has a force behind it, but whether it is conscious or unconscious is unclear to me, and immaterial, really. If there is a sense of purpose to it, I don't understand what it is. I certainly don't think God, however you define him, is concerned with my particular relations to the world. And I realize I am happy enough to live with the mystery of what life's purpose might be."

In somewhat starker terms, Nancy Gallin makes the case for there being no discernible purpose in nature whatsoever other than what humans themselves wrest from the chaos. "The purpose of life is very clear to me: it is to make the world better for other people, to love, and to work. That's it. I tell my children, 'I would like each of you to make some contribution, to serve the cause of justice, and to be compassionate.' But you know how people go to Yosemite and are overwhelmed by its beauty and say there must be a God? Well, I went to Yosemite and I was struck by the opposite, by the feeling that there was no connection between this beauty and human purpose, only that it exists and we exist. There is a cemetery in the park," she went on, "and we went to visit it and we saw the grave of a little girl who had cut her foot and bled to death. That was the lesson I took away: you slip on a rock and you die amid all this beauty."

The necessity of a context in which, as Wendy Kaufman put it, the "accident" of life could take place is the subject of a children's book by William Steig called *Yellow and Pink*. Like many of Steig's books, it is a philosophical rumination, but whereas his more typical subject might be human loyalty, affection, or definition of character, here he takes on the origins of life itself. In a conceit that owes as much to Charlie Chaplin as to Samuel Beckett, he convenes a conversation between "Two small figures made of wood . . . lying out in the sun one day, on an old newspaper. One was short, fat and painted pink; the other was straight, thin and painted yellow. It was hot and quiet, and they were both wondering."

"Do you happen to know what we're doing here?" asked Yellow.
"No," said Pink. "I don't even remember getting here."

The conversation soon turns to how they came to be lying in the sun in the middle of a fine meadow.

Pink looked Yellow over. He found Yellow's color, his well chiseled head, his whole form, admirable. "Someone must have made us," he said.
"How could anyone make something like me, so intricate, so perfect?" Yellow asked. "Or for that matter, like you? And wouldn't we know who made us, since we had to be there when we got made?
"And why," Yellow added, "would he leave us like this— with no explanation. I say we're an accident, somehow or other we just happened."
Pink couldn't believe what he heard; he started laughing. "You mean these arms I can move this way and that, this head I can turn in any direction, this breathing nose, these walking feet, all of this just happened, by some kind of fluke? That's preposterous!"

The two jointed figures then engage in a debate about how they came to be. On Pink's side is all the power of visceral certainty, the implacable logic of a first cause. On Yellow's is a ludicrous suspension of disbelief, a vision of evolution that reflects not molecular accretion and the pull and tug of environmentally sensitive organisms but a Rube Goldberg series of wholly improbable accidents.
" 'Well, it could be something like this,' " suggests an anxiously pacing Yellow to a blithely recumbent Pink.

"Suppose a branch broke off a tree and fell on a sharp rock in just the right way, so that one end split open and made legs. So there you have legs.

"Then winter came and this piece of wood froze and the ice split the mouth open. There's your mouth."

The dialogue continues, with Pink insisting on design and Yellow on happenstance, until Yellow acknowledges, " 'I can't answer all the questions. Some things will have to remain a mystery. Maybe forever. But why are we arguing on such a fine day?' "

Just then a man who needed a haircut came shambling along, humming out of tune.

He picked up Pink and looked him over. Then he picked up Yellow and looked him over. "Nice and dry," he said.

He tucked them both under his arm and headed back where he'd come from.

"Who is this guy?" Yellow whispered in Pink's ear.

Pink didn't know.

The first time I came across *Yellow and Pink,* I reacted as if I had been handed a loudly ticking package. I read it through quickly, then guiltily shoved it back on the bookstore shelf. However fond of the author, I was not about to bring *this* Steig home to Anna, and I defended myself from the charge of censorship with some rationalizing twist of conscience I can no longer recall. Like some Creationist stopping up his ears at the mention of the fossil record, I did not want to have to deal with an argument at once so simple and seductive and so inimical to my own sense of life's complexity and mystery.

A year or so later, by the time her second-grade class got around to reading *Yellow and Pink* as part of their celebration of "William Steig Month," my anxiety that

Anna would be so easily seduced had been allayed by the evidence of her natural skepticism, which consistently took the form of asking the next question: How do people know? It was a skepticism shared, as it turned out, by most of her classmates, for whom *Yellow and Pink* served primarily as a springboard to further speculation about first causes and origins of many kinds. In the course of discussion that followed the reading of the story, the class had compiled a list of questions under the heading "I Wonder," by which they meant questions for which there were no certain answers. The list began, appropriately enough, with "Who was the first person in the world?" and continued through "How many universes are there? Does the universe ever end? How was the world made? Is there really a God? Is there really heaven?"

What struck me most when I came upon the list on a visit to the classroom was the absence of certainty, or even the expectation of certainty, it reflected, the assumption apparently shared by these children—probably half of whom were getting some form of religious instruction—that there are things beyond knowing in all categories. Unlike those of us struggling to reconcile old and new cosmologies, they were coming at the big questions fresh and unblinkered. They were not unnerved by the mysteries, nor did they rush to name them or assign them extraordinary powers. "I don't feel frightened by not knowing things," the physicist Richard Feynman once told an interviewer, "by being lost in a mysterious universe without any purpose, which is the way it really is, so far as I can tell. It doesn't frighten me." Like Feynman, these children were at home in mystery, and it didn't frighten them.

Chapter 2

GOD

Elizabeth Ann said to her Nan:
"Please will you tell me how God began?
Somebody must have made Him. So
Who could it be, 'cos I want to know?"
And Nurse said, "Well!"
And Ann said, "Well?
I know you know, and I wish you'd tell."
And Nurse took pins from her mouth, and said,
"Now then, darling, it's time for bed."

Elizabeth Ann
Had a wonderful plan:
She would run round the world till she found a man
Who knew *exactly* how God began.

She got up early, she dressed, and ran
Trying to find an Important Man.
She ran to London and knocked at the door
Of the Lord High Doodelum's coach-and-four.
"Please, sir (if there's anyone in),
However-and-ever did God begin?"

The Lord High Doodelum lay in bed,
But out of the window, large and red,
Came the Lord High Coachman's face instead.
And the Lord High Coachman laughed and said:
"Well, what put *that* in your quaint little head?"

Elizabeth Ann went home again
And took from the ottoman Jennifer Jane.
"Jennifer Jane," said Elizabeth Ann,
"Tell me *at once* how God began."
And Jane, who didn't much care for speaking,
Replied in her usual way by squeaking.

What did it mean? Well, to be quite candid,
I don't know, but Elizabeth Ann did.
Elizabeth Ann said softly, "Oh!
Thank you, Jennifer. Now I know."

—"Explained" by A. A. Milne

For a subject of such presumably ubiquitous interest, how children form their individual notions of God has received remarkably little attention as a psychological phenomenon. Parents whose psychological enlightenment begins and ends with Freud, for example, are liable to be mystified by the strength and persistence of the "illusion" whose speedy expiration he predicted over a half century ago, while virtually any educated modern parent will be at least vaguely aware that religion and a belief in God are somehow considered psychologically suspect. Neurotic, infantile, and regressive are among the most common pejoratives for dispositions that were once the human norm and, in terms of their sheer numbers, remain so. Indeed, despite our everyday familiarity with such notions as projection—including Freud's rephrasing of Genesis to the effect that "man made God in his own image"—and despite the virtual dismantling of traditional theology and the transformation of the Bible over the last century and a half from literal truth to metaphorical guide, millions of people continue to share what William James described as "a perception of what we may call 'something there,' more deep and more general than any of the special and particular 'senses,' " and millions of children continue to invest their imaginations in a patriarchal figure whose cultural rigidity makes many of their elders extremely uneasy. Why is this so, and how does it happen? Where do children get their ideas of God?

It was unquestionably easier once upon a time. When I attended parochial school in the 1950s, God had a definite shape, sex, and powers, uncontested skin tone, and apparently universal franchise. His image could be found on laminated plaques and holy cards, his name was invoked by contestants in war, in love, and in volleyball. There were answers in print for every conceivable Big Question and they all began with—or came around in the end to—an omnipotent, eternal, and all-wise God. Jews discovered him in the Torah and the Talmud, Protestants in the Bible, Catholics in the drama of the Mass and the pages of the Baltimore Catechism.

Beginning with Question Number One, "Who made you?" and its answer, "God made me," the catechism employed a mock-Socratic method that was as hypnotic as it was certain in its effect, settling in rapid sequence, and with a finality that was at once arrogant and comforting, the central and trickiest mysteries of faith.

Why did God make you?
   God made me to know Him, to love Him and to serve Him.
Who is God?
   God is the Creator of heaven and earth and of all things.
What kind of a being is God?
   God is a pure spirit, infinitely perfect.
Was God always?
   God always was, is now, and always will be; He is eternal.

All discussions aimed at the amplification of this portrait were by definition circular—that is, no matter the question or its phrasing, the answer ultimately conformed to the received word. God was God. And though as Catholics we did not much think about what other denominations believed—or, rather, we tended to discount it—it turned out that God was plain God for them too, the very God of the Pledge of Allegiance and the dollar bill, of baseball, of sneezes and being spared by hurricanes that inexplicably flattened the next town over.

Then, just as the first of the baby-boom generation began graduating from high school, God was pronounced dead, not by the Russians or my favorite renegade Catholic, Madalyn Murray O'Hair, but by an interdenominational sampling of theologians whose long-private debate on the nature of the divine was abruptly catapulted into the popular press as news. "Nietzsche's thesis," ran the April 8, 1966, story in *Time*, "was that striving, self-centered man had killed God, and that settled that. The current death of God group believes that God is indeed absolutely dead, but proposes to carry on and write a theology without *theos,* without God. Less radical Christian thinkers hold that at the very least, God in the image of man, God sitting in heaven, is dead, and—in the central task of religion today—they seek to imagine and define a God who can touch man's emotions and engage men's minds."

The faithful at large did not subscribe to such a view, though ultimately they would suffer its effects. Reflecting a centuries-old chasm between ordinary believers and professionals, the Harris poll of the previous year, 1965, reported that 97 percent of the American people said they believed in God (though only 22 percent called themselves

"deeply religious," and only 44 percent attended church
or synagogue weekly). Twenty-five years later, those figures are virtually unchanged. That is, when asked the
simple question, "Do you believe in God?" somewhere
between 94 and 96 percent of the total adult population
will, on any given day late in the twentieth century, answer, "Yes."

But if pollsters were to press respondents to describe
the God they have in mind, it would quickly become
clear that anything even approximating a consensus as to
God's person, nature, or powers is out of the question.
While definitions such as that offered by Gallup in one
of its surveys—"a supreme being who created the earth
and who rewards and punishes everyone on it"—continue to reflect the majority view, phrases like "governing
force" and "higher power" are necessary to bridge the
gap for an increasing number of believers. The sheer fre-
quency of the temperature-taking, meanwhile, suggests
something like a national case of hypochondria on the
subject. Do we or don't we (still) believe? How fervently?
How specifically? Are we still a nation under God?

Given such widespread but greatly personalized belief,
the issue for most parents is not whether they believe in
God, but how they hope to describe the God in whom
they believe to their children. Will it be a revisionist She
or the ancient He, a black God, a white God, or one
tactfully disembodied and color-free? Will it be the all-
powerful, all-knowing Creator of the Old and New Testaments, or a disinterested and genderless First Cause who
long ago set everything in motion but who cannot be
held responsible for the things that go terribly wrong in
life, like earthquakes, birth defects, and fatal viruses? Is

he out *there* somewhere, watching and judging, or is he the shared consciousness and conscience within? Does he have a plan, and if so, how do we figure in it?

For many of the parents I talked to, the problem begins here, in the obligation to define, for an interviewer or a child, something so nearly inarticulable. It is not a trick question, only a hard one, and, over and over, parents prefaced their attempts to describe the God of their adult belief by saying, "Well, it's *not* the man with the white beard sitting on a throne." Or as one mother said, "I guess everybody has given up on the white-haired guy."

That said, then what? Well, "the good within us" is popular, along with its variant, "the thing that is best in me." "First Cause," "a sense of oneness," "a higher power," and "the universal order" were also invoked frequently, if tentatively. "God is internal," said a woman who had grown up without belief but liked the idea. "The thing inside you that drives you toward good works." And another friend, sweeping her arm wide to include all that she sees from where we are sitting, asks, "How can you not believe there is a God?"—then confesses to having nothing terribly clear in mind herself. From such inchoate gropings to a God one can share enthusiastically with one's children requires a willed and dextrous leap of imagination—or a surrender to somebody else's approved version.

For some of the parents I interviewed, to speak of God's existence as only a possibility is as peculiar a notion as its opposite is to nonbelievers. It is a conviction integral to their sense of the world and its ordering. But even among those who believe deeply, belief tends to be described more in terms of need or an interpretive choice than of some absolute abstraction. "I choose to believe," is how my sister Mary describes her faith. "I have always liked the idea from Saint Augustine that we are never satisfied, no matter what we have achieved, and that is what keeps us striving for more—the sense that we are without. We are not complete until we reach God."

In a similar expression of the indispensability of faith, my friend Constance Beavon turned to me at the end of a long Sunday morning service at the Episcopalian church that is a big part of her family's life and said, "I don't know how anyone gets through the week without this." It was not the rapture of the zealot but the grateful fervor of the truly comforted. And the comfort was not simply in the graceful lines of the Renwick nave or the cadence of the seventeenth-century hymns sung by choir and congregation, the aesthetically rich "devices of ritual" (in Constance's phrase) that set the stage for the spiritual plunge one comes to church in hopes of taking. It was in the immutable conviction that the plunge is worth taking, that at bottom one will discover what one seeks to find—redemption, renewal, hope, transcendence. Thus she describes her own belief very much in terms of the classic leap of faith, which is to say that she chooses, by some combination of will and instinct, to interpret the experiences of a lifetime "in such a way that I am led to belief in something that is, after all, quite unlikely."

Belief so pursued becomes a state of being and consciousness that one inhabits, much as one inhabits one's own skin or culture. Such faith has its emotional equivalent not in the shaky ambivalence of the many who once believed but now wonder, mourn, or regret, but in the congenital unbeliever, as it were, the adult raised from infancy without a God—his psychological circuitry never having been imprinted with the certainty that is the birthright and starting point for many believers.

To someone raised without belief, it is faith itself that appears unfathomable—something one must be born into to comprehend. "I don't remember ever believing in God," said Nancy Gallin. "But I didn't feel deprived of anything because of it." In fact, among the many lifelong atheists I interviewed, though several articulated their position as a rational advance over belief, and a few others confessed to wishing, at least on occasion, that they had been endowed with faith by their parents, most described it as simply one of the many random givens of their lives, on the order of hair color or height: an unchangeable fact, and one with considerable reach but only a fact. If they claimed losses at all, they tended to measure them in terms of not belonging, or of having to do without the illusory joys of certitude rather than for any deeply felt sense of having been spiritually shortchanged.

There is, for example, in Ronnie McFadden's description of herself as a "red diaper" baby—a child of left-wing or Communist parents—neither complaint not longing for some more conventional past. "My parents were very clearly atheists," she says, "first-generation Jews who were aware of prejudice but took it as cultural. We were the only ones in our neighborhood to not give some vague observance to religion. It didn't bother me a bit as a child. It was the way things were."

Robin Glazer, on the other hand, a red-diaper baby of similar vintage, and a mother of five, would not have minded being purposefuly indoctrinated one way or another. When she was growing up in a housing project in

Queens, New York, religion meant socialist summer camp and political activism. "That's what I thought Jews did," she says. And although the family did not attend synagogue, the children were never allowed to say they didn't believe in God, leaving them in a curiously ambivalent position from the outset. "I think my mother felt, why tempt fate? Which is interesting because that's about the position my kids take now. The philosophy in this house, among the kids, is, 'We don't believe or anything—but what if it's true?'

"If someone had taught me that God was there and had given me all the rituals to go with it," she says, "I would have been happy to go along. But how can you believe in God if you weren't taught to believe in him?"

To be raised without belief, on the other hand, does not imply a lack of interest in the subject. Kaari Ward remembers a fair amount of discussion about "whether there was a God" when she was a child. "My father, who had been raised Russian Orthodox in Estonia, said he did not necessarily believe in God but he believed in man's spirituality. My mother, who had been raised as a Lutheran, was really the nonbeliever. She was extremely rational and it fit her personality. I didn't miss being a believer until I got to college. Then I discovered all my good friends talking about religion and rejecting it, and I had nothing to reject."

Jan Miller was also raised in a nonbelieving family. She remembers how "when my sister found out in high school that her best friend was a believer, it had the force of a revelation. She came home and said, 'You know, Susie believes there is a God as much as I believe there isn't one!' " When Miller herself came to a position of faith as an adult, her family was polite but mystified. "Is it like having a sixth sense?" Miller's mother asked her.

At some point in our conversation, Robin Glazer made reference to the fact that she had yet to suffer any major losses in her life—her parents were still alive, her children were all healthy, and it was easy, she said, for her and her husband to maintain the illusion that the world was a safe and manageable place, God or no God. But for Danya and Tamar Kraft-Stolar, two young sisters whose mother, Veronika, died of cancer at forty-two, it was clear that the issue of belief versus nonbelief posed a more intimate challenge. Having been raised as atheists, like their parents before them, both of them found it hard to imagine the personal God in whom many of their friends believed. At the same time, they confessed to being attracted by the appearance of an answer for something that made no real sense.

"I don't believe in God," Danya said at fifteen, "but sometimes I would like to. It would make everything so simple. If you believed that God was everlasting, then— I'd love to think that there was a heaven, or something. But I don't. I can't really imagine believing, so I don't know what it's like."

"I would like to believe that there's a reason for everyone who has died," said Tamar, who was twelve at the time. "But I can't. And I hate it when people say, 'It's because God wanted it that way.' I think they're very insecure with the question and they just don't know what to say. Like there's got to be a reason for everything."

"Doesn't it comfort them?" her father asked.

"It just doesn't comfort me," Tamar replied.

For parents who have no belief themselves, providing

a God for their children would seem a difficulty beyond surmounting. Yet a surprisingly large number of the nonbelieving parents I interviewed confessed themselves reluctant to tell their children outright that they did not believe in God, or that they doubted his existence. For most, the question represented a true conflict between their powerful feelings of not wanting to lie to their children ("I read somewhere that lying to your child about what you believe is the only sin," one parent told me) and their suspicion that their children's need for God might be more important at a given moment than the parent's scruples. It is one thing to come to terms with your own disbelief—or to think you have—and another thing entirely to pass it on. As one woman, herself raised a Catholic, put it, "My eight-year-old son says, 'You don't believe in God, do you?' and I say, 'Not a God who is a person.' But when he says, 'I don't believe in God,' I get a feeling in the pit of my stomach."

Still others are able to separate their own beliefs from what they think appropriate to tell children. Speaking of his then three-year-old daughter's need to believe in a God she had formed out of cultural references and her own imagination, the writer Jules Feiffer, an atheist, said, "I wouldn't say to Halley, 'There is no God.' I would say to her, 'This is what a lot of people think. Grandpa thinks this, other people think that. This is what Daddy thinks.' As you grow older, God becomes a rigid image, more hard-nosed, more mixed up with your parents and your need to rebel against them. But when you are younger, it has to do with your imagination and your idealization of your parents and your wanting to be good—all of which are important to development."

And all of which proceeds, in any event, with or without parental cooperation. Children raised without religious instruction, or without parents who believe, discover God in the playground and at nursery school, absorb him by way of babysitters and friends, have their awareness of him reinforced by movies, television, and the casual profanity of the street. He is, indeed, everywhere, and parents who suggest otherwise are often surprised by the intensity with which their children insist on God's reality.

Sarah Lang, an ex-Catholic whose own "longing to be spiritual" has gone painfully unsatisfied in adult life, started out by telling her older daughter, Emily, then about four, what she honestly thought. "Because I don't have a belief, I told her I didn't think there was a God, but she was furious at me.

"Now I say I believe because that's so clearly what she wants to hear," Sarah says. "And," she adds, voicing that sense of guilt mixed with loss that many former believers feel, "because I feel I impoverish her by my unbelief."

When her daughter Sophie was about four, Penny Coleman, a photographer who was raised Episcopalian but is now a nonbeliever, began referring to the God Sophie and her older brother Charlie brought home as a "she." "Sophie was furious. 'He's *not* a she,' she would insist." But when Sophie was five, Penny took her to an exhibit at a local gallery where one of the works of art was a room in which a freestanding arrangement of transparent plastic stelae rose from a floor crisscrossed with blinking electric lights. "Sophie stood there for a while transfixed," Penny says, "and then she said, 'It's God.' " Her mother did not feel inclined to correct her.

Dan Polin had a similar reaction to a question his son Ben put to him as the two of them walked home from an Easter service at a local Catholic church. They had gone because Dan, a "quasi-religious, nonobserving former Jew married to a former Catholic," likes to stop into church occasionally, but they had become restless and left early. As they were waiting at a corner for the light to change, Ben suddenly turned to his father and asked, "Why didn't you name me Jesus?"

"Well, frankly," Dan said, "it never occurred to us. Do you wish we had called you Jesus?" "Yes," said Ben, who was about to turn six. When Dan asked him why, he explained, "So I can be the son of God."

"My interpretation of this," said Dan later, "was that he wanted to be someone important, and so I said to him, 'I think you want to grow up to be somebody important, don't you?' And he kind of nodded. So when we got home, I of course told Eileen about this, but her reaction, as someone who had been raised Catholic, was quite different, which was very interesting to me. She immediately said to Ben, 'Well, you *are* God's son. We are all God's children.' "

Coexisting with the willingness of most children to go along with the general assumption that God exists and is happily known to all are their various unsocialized opinions or observations about God and his powers that tend to focus on the fuzziness or incongruity of this uniquely important figure—the sort of "oops" remarks that the old Art Linkletter show used to specialize in.

"How did you know you were God?" reads one of the scrawled entries in the popular *Children's Letters to God*. And another: "Instead of letting people die and haveing

GOD   57

[sic] to make new ones why don't you just keep the ones
you got now?" Or: "Dear God, How come you did all
those miracles in the old days and don't do any now?"
There is, quite understandably, something of "The Emperor's New Clothes" in children's attempts to solve the
riddle. And a degree of imprecision equal to that shown
by their elders. "God?" one eleven-year-old Catholic
began uncertainly when I asked her if she could describe
him for me. "He's not really a human, I guess. I don't
know what he looks like, just a big person who can do
whatever he wants and is perfect." And from a nonbelieving counterpart, aged twelve, a politic hedge that is
one-half Pascal, one-half adolescent superstition: "I don't
believe there is a guy up there, or a woman up there,
who just appeared one day and created the earth. But if
I say that, then if there is something up there, it'll get
mad at me. So I just really don't say it, if I can help it."

The irresistible question, given the great diversity of
opinion and nervousness about its answer, is of course
straight from the Catechism, by way of Milne. What kind
of being *is* God—and however did he begin?

The question first occurred to Ana-Maria Rizzuto, a
psychoanalyst and professor of psychiatry, almost thirty
years ago, as she was preparing a course for seminarians
on the "psychological foundations of belief and pastoral
care." In researching the literature, Rizzuto discovered
that no clinical studies of the phenomenon had ever been
conducted, that in fact no theory existed that might explain how children actually form their images of God.

"Freud," she writes in *The Birth of the Living God,*
"offered brilliant insights into the role of the parents in
the formation of the representation of God. Jung accu-

mulated complex elaborations about religion, symbols, archetypes, and the archetype of the self. Adler converted God into a value. Other analysts have elaborated aspects of Freud's or Jung's ideas, but I found no extensive clinical studies at hand to assist me. . . . The most complete were Gesell's systematic obervations of the child's interest in God and children, but he did not correlate these with the child's subjective experience. In summary, existing studies contributed to a description of an observable process but threw no light on the secret, unconscious weavings of images, feelings, and ideation which converge in the childhood process of elaborating a representation of God."

In pursuit of those "secret, unconscious weavings," Rizzuto undertook a pilot study of patients at Boston State Hospital in the mid-1960s. "We had been treating patients for years," she writes, "without listening systematically to their expressed desires for closeness to God or avoidance of him. I reasoned that if Freud was correct, if God is, in fact, an 'exaltation' of parental imagos, our ignorance of God's psychic role in an individual's life meant missing an important and relevant piece of information about the patient's developmental history. . . ."

Taking Freud as her point of departure, but drawing extensively upon subsequent reworkings of his theories, and particularly the work of the British object-relations school, Rizzuto proceeds to construct an immensely intricate, fascinating, and largely persuasive theory of how children construct their initial "God-representations" and how and why those representations change over time, increasing or diminishing in psychic importance.

She begins with Freud's repeatedly stated position that gods and demons "are creations of the human mind" based on "revivals and restorations of the young child's ideas" of his father and mother. "Psychoanalysis," Freud argued in the 1910 paper on Leonardo da Vinci from which Rizzuto quotes, "has made us familiar with the intimate connexion between the father-complex and belief in God; it has shown us that a personal God is, psychologically, nothing other than an exalted father. . . . Thus we recognize that the roots of the need for religion are in the parental complex; the almighty and just God, and kindly Nature, appear to us as grand sublimations of father and mother, or rather as revivals and restorations of the young child's ideas of them."

While acknowledging Freud's essential contribution toward "finding out *how* the idea of gods and devils had come into existence in the human mind," Rizzuto points to the many loose threads he overlooked in his analysis, among them the problem of how the Oedipus complex plays out in the young girl's conception of God, "the fact that there must be a critical psychological difference between religious believers and nonbelievers," and the usefulness of the " 'revived' and 'restored' ideas of the parents in later life." He neglects as well, she writes, "to expore further the persistence of belief and its many functions in everyday life."

In pursuit of these several unexplored issues, Rizzuto picks her way through a dense thicket of post-Freudian theory before reaching the clearing of D. W. Winnicott's "transitional space," a sort of demilitarized zone that Winnicott locates "outside, inside, and at the the border" of the psyche—a territory that comes into existence at the moment the infant first begins to distinguish between self and mother, between illusion and reality.

It is within this zone that children engage in necessary

creative play, freely mixing fantasy and reality—the raw materials of myth—and here they create or discover what Winnicott terms "transitional objects"—the teddy bears, thumbs, favorite pieces of clothing, imaginary companions—which are invested with special properties by the child and which serve as comforting stand-ins for the mother during the protracted process of separation. In this space and in this manner, the healthy child creates his own source of security and comfort: his "Linus" blanket, his teddy bear—private, portable, personal.

From the adult point of view, Winnicott argues, the transitional object appears to come "from without . . . but not so from the point of view of the baby. Neither does it come from within; it is not a hallucination." "I am staking a claim," he writes, "for an intermediate state between a baby's inability and his growing ability to recognize and accept reality. I am therefore studying the substance of *illusion,* that which is allowed to the infant, and which in adult life is inherent in art and religion."

"We can share a respect for illusory experience," he writes, "and if we wish we may collect together and form a group on the basis of the similarity of our illusory experiences. This is a natural root of grouping among human beings."

The distinction between Freud's view of illusion and Winnicott's is essential to Rizzuto's location of God in this intermediate zone. For Freud, illusion is a wishful and ultimately damaging contradiction of reality, a substitution of wishes for reality in the attempt to fulfill human needs or placate human fears; for Winnicott, illusion is a creative participation in, and a healthy shaping of, reality. In Rizzuto's formulation, then, to identify the God of the child as, "psychologically speaking . . . an illusory transitional object" is to rescue him from the psychoanalytic dustbin and place him atop the toy box. Not God in his heaven, perhaps, but at least under the roof again—a metaphysical Velveteen Rabbit in whom the child is free to invest his most exalted or comforting notions and whose bare outline is fleshed out over time with attributes supplied by the larger culture—the personal and private made communal and universal.

This transitional object-God is thus a hybrid figure, pieced together from a variety of personal and cultural "representations." Each child's personal God owes his existence, appearance, character, and powers to an assortment of early influences and images—that of the loving (or cold) mother, the protecting (or punishing) father, the pious (or obsessive) grandmother, the optimistic nursemaid, and so on—all further fleshed out with the features of the God described by the larger culture. One consequence of this theistic carpentering, of course, is that in terms of significant qualities, the God described by any two believers is likely to be as varied as the father or mother described by different siblings. Some are splendid, some deserving of renunciation, some barely present. The God of Ingmar Bergman is surely not the God of Anthony Trollope, the God of Jimmy Swaggert not the God of Cardinal O'Connor, the God of Rabbi Harold Kushner (*When Bad Things Happen to Good People*) not the God of Hannah Arendt.

At the same time, the power of the received cultural image remains enormous, capable of overriding the most intensely felt personal imagery. In *A Good Enough Parent,*

Bruno Bettelheim observes that "hardly any modern child thinks of God in any other form than that of a most exalted, immortal, very old person. As we mature, for most of us this image is replaced by the abstract idea of a formless supreme being, or essence, or first cause, as the case may be. Nevertheless, we continue to admire how God was rendered in human form by great artists, such as Michelangelo did in the depiction of the creation of Adam on the ceiling of the Sistine Chapel. And in some such form God appears to us in our dreams, which suggests that however far we have removed ourselves from our childish imagery, in our unconscious it continues as we had visualized it and thought of it as children."

The durability of that Renaissance God is something Lynn Westfield, the director of religious education at Riverside Church in New York, must contend with all the time. She tells the story of how during a Sunday school session she conducted one morning, she invited a group of mostly African-American children to say what they thought God might look like. Despite Westfield's pointed suggestions to the effect that God might be female, might be some color other than white, might even be totally disembodied, one child after another responded by describing the Caucasian God depicted in stained glass windows and traditional religious art. Finally, as Westfield was about to give up, one boy shyly offered an alternative. "Bill Cosby?" he said.

In fact, argues Rizzuto, "no child in the Western world brought up in ordinary circumstances completes the Oedipal cycle without forming at least a rudimentary God-representation, which he may use for belief or not." And unless emphatically contradicted by parents, whatever private portrait the child paints for himself becomes more real and more credible for its continual reinforcement by the surrounding society.

' "The child," Rizzuto observes, "hears people talk respectfully about God. There are special people—ministers, priests, rabbis—who represent him officially. They speak a solemn language with special intonations of gravity, and address themselves to God. The child sees special buildings, pieces of art, celebrations—all of which have to do with the 'big person' called God. In most families the parents defer to God and worship him or else give indications that they are different from other parents because they do *not* believe in God. . . .

"Most importantly, God is referred to as real, existing, powerful, and in charge of the world. From presidents of nations and those who (in the United States) continually say 'God bless America,' to the drunken beggar who thanks one with 'God bless you,' everyone refers to God. One sneezes and God is there. One is given a nickel and God is there. One asks where this ubiquitous person is, and grown-ups solemnly assure one, 'Everywhere.' "

His "reality" thus reinforced, this individually created God takes his place in the child's inner life, "a transitional object at the service of gaining leverage with oneself, with others, and with life itself."

The concept of God as inner resource—renewable, changeable, capable of inflation or diminution, of enrichment or abstraction, as repository of ideals and comfort in crisis—bridges the gulf, psychologically if not theologically, that separates the adult who worships from the adult who cannot, the adult who prefers to keep his internal God to himself from the one who requires a God shared by many, the adult possessed of a mystifying but unrelinquishable abstraction and the child enthralled by the holy superman said to take such a personal interest in him. In a sense, that internalized God is the "best parent" to whom we all want to remain attached, and whom, if we become parents, we want to pass on to our children.

But what of the other "God," the one in whose name humans have been hacking one another to pieces for millennia, the one for whom first stones have been cast time and again, the one in whose defense "infidels" must be assailed, the one who seems to have whispered competing truths in select ears for centuries? I have a folder full of newspaper clippings referring to this God—a God too bloody for contemporary American tastes but very much with the world still. Where did this highly disagreeable God come from?

His origin is in perfect symmetry with that of the idealized and currently popular God; he is the bad-guy twin of the good-guy God, the grumpy old monosyllabic dictator father to the New Age "caring" father. It is of course this God who has been so widely rejected, as if by fiat. He is not nice and he is a lot of trouble. A great many contemporary believers deal with his unacceptability by declaring there never was such a God, only human misreadings and false claims made in his name, and they offer instead their improved and eternally benign God. When things go right, he is there to be thanked. When things go wrong, somebody else has slipped up. Or as I recall being told in a variety of circumstances, the ways of the Lord are mysterious.

Nonbelievers resolve the issue rather more radically, dispensing with God altogether. No good guy/bad guy,

only no guy. This is called throwing out the baby with
the bathwater in some circles, a clean break in others.
The most unforgiving of nonbelievers, who tend, in my
experience, not just to spring from orthodox stock but
to have been endowed at birth with a punishing scrupulousness, tend as well to remain forever resentful for
having been suckered at an early age. And who, knowing
the troubles they've seen, can fault them? "I figure the
only way to be a good Catholic," reflects a young man
driven to distraction by his and the church's mutually
negating obsessions with sex in Charles Simmons's novel
Powdered Eggs, "is to be rich, sterile, impotent, inhibitedly
queer or old." More sanguine types sound a mournful
note of regret at the collapse of a God one might like to
believe in still but cannot. Nearly thirty-five years after
book publisher Paul Fargis held the plate as an altar boy
at my First Communion, I asked him what had become
of his childhood faith and it turned out he had still not
quite made up his mind about its central figure.

"If I'm going to believe in God," he said, "then there's
a reason for earthquakes. But the only possible designer
I could believe in has to be benevolent. Not the one who
says, 'You screw around with me and I'll send the light-
ning bolt.' We're taught to forgive, but he sends you to
hell for missing mass. Some days, I'm a total nonbeliever,
and I think, 'It's amazing how for so many years people
have had this put over on them, this mythology.' Then,
other days, I think, my heart ticks away—how can there
not be a God, I'd better go back to church. The older I
get, the less reflexive I get about it. Today, Wednesday,
I really don't think it's possible to get away from one's
upbringing, but only to weather it, face it."

What Fargis and others are indirectly articulating are

the built-in limits of monotheism, the inherent difficulty of asking one God to satisfy many different human needs. The Greeks and the Romans went at it differently, splitting attributes and roles among many deities, albeit with unsatisfying results of another kind. Though monotheism continues to be viewed in the West as the great singular advance in religious and philosophical thought, in a practical sense believers have been tinkering with that supposedly one God ever since—most spectacularly with the assertion of Jesus' divinity, but more routinely and modestly by continual reinterpretation of his intent. What, after all, do doctrines like free will or predestination signify if not particular—and opposed—views of God's intent, and by implication, his very nature? The God who intends man to be truly free is a wholly different character from the God who rigs the game ahead of time, and, as history has demonstrated, the followers of the one are likely to find it easy to vilify the followers of the other—not just in good conscience but with fiery duty.

These days, the terms of the argument have shifted, from overtly doctrinal disputes to the practical working out of messy political questions that have an implied moral base: abortion, homelessness, the distribution of wealth, the protection of the planet, the right to die, the right to substitute prayer for medical treatment for one's child. Each of these is heatedly argued by ad hoc alliances drawn together without reference to official religious boundaries but rather in response to some greater and more personal moral vision—some intimately conceived God shared only by few. Thus we have the highly popular laissez-faire God—he who "helps those who help themselves"—and the vastly impractical God of Saint Luke: "Sell all that ye have and give alms."

As the son of a Baptist minister, Dale Kaufman had plenty of time as a child to reflect on the variations spun on the biblical God by a succession of spokesmen, and he admits to being "deeply suspicious of the idea of God. I think it's a product of long and deep association with the religion business, and of seeing it in all its forms. There is a compelling human need to explain our existence and I see all religions as man-made constructs to help us deal with a feeble and precarious hold on life. But I don't see a need for First Cause, and I see First Cause and morality as separate."

For most people, that remains the most radical division of all. To cleave purpose from virtue is nearly as frightening as to dispense with purpose altogether. What good is a First Cause if he, she, it did not have us in mind, and did not have in mind how we should be good? Are we not then as truly on our own as if there were no First Cause at all?

Chapter 3

ETHICS AND VIRTUE

When we are planning for posterity, we ought to
remember that virtue is not hereditary.

—Thomas Paine

It is perhaps the most commonly expressed wish of parents—rivaled only by the wish that they be happy in life—that their children be good.

They must not lie, cheat, or steal, grab one another's toys, be rude to grown-ups, say mean things to their friends, or hurt people's feelings. They must not kick, hit, or pinch, must not hog the ball on the soccer field, boast of their speed in the schoolyard or their quickness in finishing chapter books. They must hold their tongues when patronized by their elders, say please and thank you and invite to their birthday parties friends with whom they are out of sorts. They must be ever mindful of those less fortunate, must strive always to be fair, yet endure being told over and over, in contexts large and small, that life itself is not fair.

All this we demand of children so that they will become good people—like ourselves only better—their goodness achieving what our virtue and that of our ancestors inexplicably failed to. They will make peace, not war, pay their taxes in full, care for the needy, be fair stewards of the earth. They will bring children into the world with forethought and in love only, and they will care for us, their parents, to our dying day.

Among the most enduring and sincere of parental intentions, it is as well among the most intimidating and elusive in its prospect of achievement. If it is difficult to be good, or "nice," as a child, it is frequently more difficult as an adult, and that knowledge fills parents with anxiety. The process of instilling "basic values" in children, a responsibility long shared by parents with the larger community, with schools and religious institutions, seems to many modern parents to devolve almost exclusively to them, obliging them to prevail, somehow, and in essential isolation, against the nonexistent or warring standards of a society in a constant state of flux, or, as direr prophets have it, utter collapse.

" 'Selfishness,' 'me-ism,' 'yuppie greed'—the usual characterizations of our malaise—do not describe very clearly what ails us," wrote Christopher Lasch in an essay marking the end of the 1980s. "The moral bottom has dropped out of our culture . . . [leaving] young people in our society . . . in a state of almost unbearable, though inarticulate, agony." To raise a moral child, a good and virtuous child, seems a peculiarly precarious and lonely affair in modern life. Not only is a successful outcome always in doubt, but an unhappy one is almost certain to be attributed to parental failure.

Our personal sense of impending disaster is correspondingly acute. In the course of a long talk I had recently with a friend whose husband was dying, the question of how his death would affect their eleven-year-old son came up repeatedly. We talked about the son's difficulty in expressing his fears about his father's illness,

of how much he loves his father and how wonderful their
relationship has been, of how deprived he is going to be
by his father's death, of how cruelly sad the anticipation
of all this is, both for the parent who will survive it and
the one who will die knowing it. Having gone through
the experience with a much younger child, I tried to be
reassuring, but was not doing very well when, picturing
the child in question, a sweet, friendly boy who loves
sports and his parents, I suddenly asked my friend, "What
is your worst fear for Daniel?" To which my friend—
intelligent, solvent, resourceful, and personally kind—
answered without hesitation, "That he'll become a ju-
venile delinquent."

Even taking into account the temporary irrationality
of a mother taxed by dread and anticipatory grief, it struck
me as a wild anxiety. How could she imagine such a
transformation in her beloved son? (In fact, as my daughter's father was dying, my worst projection for her—she
was then in first grade, about to turn six—was that she
would not learn to read, a failure I imagined triggering
a lifelong series of tragic failures. Buried in that equally
irrational anxiety, I suppose, was an assumption equivalent to my friend's—that her future was going to be
ruined by this awful turn in her young life.)

Do my friend and I—do we all, perhaps—believe that
our children hover so close to the brink? A single loss
too big, a misstep unforeseen and it's into the forest with
William Golding's boys? On the subject of the frailty of
the human race, and its natural inclination to wickedness,
there has certainly never been a shortage of pessimism,
within organized religion or without. Just as our ultimate
helplessness as parents inspires scenarios of improbable

physical catastrophe—what parent can forestall the ca-reening taxi, outwit deranged white cells, anticipate fall-ing masonry in the next block?—so does it inspire fears for our children's moral safety once they pass beyond our control.

Behind much of this parental angst over children's moral development lies a conflicting pair of beliefs. On the one hand is the powerful conviction expressed by nearly every parent I spoke to that morality is an inherent trait in us all, that humans do innately know the difference between right and wrong and can be persuaded to act cheerfully on that understanding except under intolerable conditions of deprivation. "I think that people do know what's right and what's wrong," said one mother, "even when they are doing something wrong, even if they can't stop themselves." Competing with this benign vision is the nearly overwhelming sense that an insistence on vir-tue, or morality, however you might define it, is a lost cause, that one's own efforts are as sand thrown at a charging beast. These warring certainties, the polarized residue of centuries of mutually negating philosophical speculations as to the nature of man—he is good, he is evil—now overlaid with half-comprehended psycholog-ical "truths" and salted with American optimism, not surprisingly addle the adult reckless or brave enough to think twice about the subject.

"Men are not gentle creatures who want to be loved and who at the most can defend themselves when at-tacked," Freud wrote in *Civilization and Its Discontents.* "They are on the contrary creatures among whose in-stinctual endowments is to be reckoned a powerful share of aggressiveness." It is an assessment in absolute practical harmony with the heirs of Moses and of Christ, with the dourest observers of human nature or the most optimistic: we are sinners all.

It is equally in harmony with most parents' intimate experience of their offspring. Whatever fantasies of children's native goodness one might have indulged before becoming a parent are as nothing against the evidence of an afternoon by the sandbox. However soft-cheeked and sweet-smelling, however transmutable, ultimately, into creatures of compassion and empathy, children are not born to cooperation or sacrifice but to the rawest self-interest. Curbing that aggressiveness, channeling it, re-directing it toward more fruitful pursuits, has been the spottily successful labor of society as a whole, the process (often deeply resented) we call "civilizing." It is the process meant to produce at least a majority of citizens obedient to the law: adults who neither litter nor run red lights, who return library books unmarked and on time, who pay their taxes and leave their neighbors' cars, lawn mowers, and mailboxes intact. It is a process greatly abetted by the force of law and the forces of economics, but though it regularly brushes up against larger moral issues, it does not depend on a common moral universe, nor on a common understanding of virtue or of ethical behavior. And even at its most successful, it neither sharpens conscience nor softens the heart.

For that, something quite different is necessary, some moral comprehension that transcends convention, convenience, and, in the opinion of many I talked to, organized religion. For those who aspire to more than keeping their offspring out of jail—whether for dealing drugs or skirting SEC regulations—some overarching philosophy is required, some idea of life's meaning that, as Sally Shea put it, "makes you look outside yourself, to see that there is more to life than money and material possessions."

Though commonly summed up under the reassuring terms "basic values" or "common standards,' what that "more" ought to consist of is not all that clear. Whose basic values do we mean to instill, after all, whose standards, whose virtues? When we say "good," do we mean compliance or deep conviction, niceness or backbone? Do we mean manners or decency, respectability or human regard, traditional piety or a tradition of tolerance? Do we mean teenagers who will hold their sexual impulses in check or teenagers who will take care not to become pregnant? We live in a society that is said to have "lost its moral bearings," but in fact it is a society that rests lopsidedly on a number of rival moral bedrocks, a society in which well-meaning people fervently disagree about what is moral, what is virtuous.

Two days after New York City's 1991 decision to make condoms available to junior and senior high school students in hopes of slowing the spread of AIDS among teenagers, I spoke by chance on the telephone to a woman I had never met but whose children attend the same public elementary school as my daughter. The subject of the Board of Education's vote on the issue had been intensively covered in the local press, and the debate itself had been cast in distinctly moral terms. Those opposed spoke principally of upholding a standard of sexual morality for young people, and of declining to endorse premarital sex and promiscuity by what they argued would constitute its de facto acceptance. Those in favor addressed a different moral issue, that of adult and governmental responsibility to protect sexually active teenagers (and their potential offspring) from their own negligence and ignorance. The seven-member Board of Education appeared as deeply divided as the larger public down to the day of the vote, and in fact the vote stood at three to three when the seventh member of the board, Dr. Westina L. Matthews, began to speak. A deeply religious woman whose father was a minister, she kept hundreds of onlookers in suspense as she described her own painful struggle to make the right moral decision. She had visited a health clinic in a local high school to talk to teenagers; she had consulted with the health department about the number of HIV-infected babies born each year; and she had prayed and fasted. Finally, though she reiterated her personal support for abstinence and her conviction that parents have a right to exclude their children from the distribution plan, she cast her vote in favor of making condoms available "for the sake of the children" who might be born infected.

It was, for New York City in 1991, a rare and remarkable confession of personal conscience, a welcome departure from the reflexive pieties of public figures. Yet the woman on the phone never mentioned Dr. Matthews. She simply expressed how appalled she was by the immorality of the outcome. "I can't believe this is what we want to tell young people," she said. As politely as I could, I said that I agreed with the board's decision, and on specifically moral grounds too. To which she replied without the least rancor, and only a bit of surprise, "Well, I just found out one of my closest friends feels that way too."

Certainly people of good will but opposing moral conviction have always coexisted in society, but rarely have the divisions been so idiosyncratic or so intimately juxtaposed as in contemporary America. Most of us, wherever we happen to be living at a given time, are from somewhere else, where they do things differently, and we live cheek-by-jowl with neighbors who, in turn, have been shaped by distant and unfamiliar mores. What any of us means by "good" is necessarily a mixture of abstract ethical ideals (the golden rule in its simplest form), of economic and class-influenced values, of cultural attitudes and religious beliefs, whether intact or attenuated and vestigial. "Moral relativism" is not some option chosen on achieving one's majority; it is the observable state of things.

Among my close personal friends, for example, beating a child would rank as a far greater violation of decency than adultery, a racist or anti-Semitic remark as infinitely more objectionable than a four-letter word. Behavior once regarded as morally dangerous, such as masturbation, tends now to be viewed as developmentally natural and morally neutral. And yet, to judge from the amount of hyperbolic text devoted to the subject of teenage sexual activity in the pages of Dr. James Dobson's magazine *Focus on the Family,* a great many people feel differently about these matters, and they feel it with equal fervor. "Our job as parents," one headline unequivocally blared, "is to lock and bolt the doors. . . ." To which advice my friends Constance Beavon and Bruce Saylor, weekly churchgoers whose Sunday mornings are as unalterably sacred as any subscriber of Dr. Dobson, reacted with horror. "Our job as parents," Constance replied, "is to fling open the doors as wide as possible."

The "collapse of the family," meanwhile, a long-play-ing theme among politicians and religious leaders, is spo-ken of not as a consequence or symptom of troubles abounding but as their certain cause. To a remarkable extent—and this helps explain the isolation so many claim to feel—it is an indictment that parents accept, in that they grant that they are, or ought to be, the primary molders of their children's moral character.

"We are her source of morality," said Dale Kaufman, the father of a ten-year-old. "I don't expect it to come from Sunday school, though it should obviously reinforce it. In fact," continued Kaufman, the son of a Baptist minister, "I can see no relationship between religious cul-ture and a moral code. I don't think that it in any way insures appropriate moral conduct."

While Kaufman's basic position—that parents are their children's "source of morality"—was almost universally subscribed to by the parents I talked to ("Did you ever doubt it?" one father asked), individual parents tended to assess the difficulty of carrying out this responsibility in ways seemingly unrelated to their degree of attachment or alienation from organized religion. For some, the ob-ligation is simply indistinguishable from the parental role itself. "Kids need to see it coming out of *you*," said Can-dace Burnett. "You practice it, you do it." For others, it seems far and away among the most daunting of parental challenges, one it would be unthinkable to undertake without some institutional ally. Thus Kaufman's further observation, that he saw no connection between religious culture and a moral code, would pull the rug out from under a great many already skittish people. To stand as *the* moral authority for one's children, after all, requires a confidence in one's own virtue and judgment that many parents either do not feel ("I really want a moral compass for *myself*," said one parent) or that they fear, on considerable evidence, pits them unfairly against the larger world.

"You assume," says Kaari Ward, who has raised her daughter much as she was raised by her intensely ethical but agnostic parents, "that other parents want their child to be honest too, but it turns out to be a mistaken assumption. Then you have to teach your child to negotiate in a world where not everyone is as honest as you expect her to be."

"It's difficult," says Leslie Taynor-Mones, a periodontist who lives on Long Island and is the mother of a ten-year-old. "We are teaching her how to behave as if she lived in an ideal world, but she really lives in a world that reflects almost none of the values we hold."

Though in essential agreement about the moral environment, the two women's solutions have been quite different. "I think you can give an ethical sense to children apart from religion," says Ward. "It's not easy," she added, "and you have to be consistent, but when you assign that job to a church, you run the risk of ceding your own responsibility as moral guardian. You can't just say, there is this institution over here that dispenses morality, then wash your hands of it. Parents do that with schools too, expecting them to do many of the things they need to do themselves."

By contrast, Taynor-Mones and her husband, though they do not consider themselves religious, have enrolled their daughter in a weekly class at a Reconstructionist synagogue in hopes of reinforcing the moral code they teach at home. It is a choice essentially indistinguishable from that of a lifelong believer like Jim O'Leary. Having attended a succession of suburban Ohio churches throughout his childhood—Lutheran in one community, Presbyterian and Congregationalist in another—and having been married in an Episcopal service, O'Leary simultaneously professes a credible indifference to doctrinal fine points and an unshakeable conviction about the value of taking one's children to church every week.

"I went to church every Sunday until I was eighteen," he recalls, "to school and to the service, and I think it helped me a lot. I started taking Chris [his older son] because I wanted to insure that he had a nice background, a moral background. I want him to have some idea of good versus evil, of right versus wrong. There are a whole lot of bad things out there. I want to give him the tools to choose wisely."

Though O'Leary's commitment extends to teaching his son's Sunday school class on alternate weeks, when I asked him if he observed any differences in behavior between his son and the children of his friends who did not attend church, he was, like the vast majority of parents I spoke to, quick to say that he saw none, that regardless of their church habits, the families of Chris's close friends shared similar moral attitudes. It was not his belief that all kids needed religion, he said, only that taking his son to church was something he needed to do as a father, that it represented the example he wanted his son to have. "Sunday school is what Chris and I do together."

Certainly few parents claiming to believe in the efficacy of Sunday school are as willing to back up that belief with

an equivalent commitment of time. So many would prefer the traditional morning off, it seems, that All Souls'
Unitarian-Universalist Church, a 1,400-member fellow-
ship in Manhattan with a large community outreach program, has been obliged to tell prospective members that
it is not acceptable for parents "to drop off their kids and
go home to read the paper. If it's good enough for
Muffie," explained Minister Forrester Church with a
smile, "it's good enough for her parents."

The idea that morality can somehow be taught in the
abstract, given a sufficiently clever lesson plan and a skill-
ful teacher, persists nevertheless. "A certain number of
parents," says Lynn Westfield, director of the interdenominational Riverside Church Sunday school, "look at
it as 'I take my kid to sewing, I take her to ballet, I take
her to religion. I can't do everything myself, so I take
her to the experts.' But what we do here is teach religion.
We don't give them an innoculation."

Though many parents, no doubt, do imagine that they
can guarantee some level of decency in their offspring
simply by dropping them off at the local Sunday school,
few parents I spoke with took such a cavalier attitude
toward their children's moral education. For most it was
not a matter of seeking out "the experts" to instruct their
child morally but rather of seeking out a community of
like-minded souls to reflect and reinforce a shared vision
of the moral life. What went largely unarticulated, on the
other hand, was what earlier generations would have had
no hesitation in expressing—the expectation, or, more
accurately, the conviction, that in such a community they
and their children would discover the absolute moral standard that is nowhere else to be found, and that that stan-

dard would reflect the clear will of God, the prime mover and judge of all our works.

> "As a matter of fact, the Ten Commandments were dreamed up by human beings—they just said they were from God to give the whole thing added punch. Just like when I tell my older children to tell the younger ones to be quiet, I tell them to say, '*Mommy* says.' Well, Moses came down from the mountain and said, '*God* says.' "
>
> —Nancy Gallin

However sophisticated they might be about how a moral sense is transmitted, and however willing to take a strong moral stand themselves, parents understandably long for support in the endeavor. What they want from their churches, if they are churchgoers, is very much what they want from the parents of their children's friends, from their teachers and from their neighbors—an implied guarantee that the difficult lessons they mean to teach their children will be echoed outside the home, that their authority as parents will be backed up by some consensus that will not only persuade the child but also stay with him through his inevitable later rebelliousness.

"What's good about CCD," my sister Ginny said of the Confraternity of Christian Doctrine classes her children attend, "is not so much that they are learning as that they hear it there. We talk about all the same things at home, but just as when we talk about school things at home, they don't take it as seriously as they do in school. There is an added seriousness to these issues because they hear about them elsewhere as well. And I want them to take it seriously."

"I don't have sufficient authority with Kate as it is,"
is how one friend framed the same issue. "I can complain
all I want about my Catholic upbringing and talk about
my ambivalence about religion, but there is something
to be said for a 'higher authority' located outside the
parents. I don't want Kate to have the sort of ambivalence
about me as her source of authority, that I, in effect, have
about the Church."

Finding an acceptable surrogate, or backup, to one's
exercise of parental authority turns out to be an immensely difficult task outside organized religion—however inadequate some find even that course. The
traditional places one might have looked to for support
have lost whatever moral authority they once possessed.
In the schools, teachers can no longer assume readily
agreed upon standards of behavior, while for most Americans under fifty, the various branches of government no
longer represent disinterested, legitimate authority but
have come to be seen as competing repositories of vested
interests.

But establishing their own legitimacy as authorities is
probably the most difficult task for many parents. The
habit of skepticism that came to define a generation that
passed through high school and college during the 1960s
and early 1970s has taken a toll. A woman I spoke to,
who grew up Catholic in Wyoming and now lives in a
small town in the Pacific Northwest, looks back on some
of her choices as a "flower-child parent" with dismay.
"You know how they used to say about our generation,
that we never suffered, that we were spoiled rotten, dil-
ettantes, and so on. Well, I keep thinking, wait till they
see the generation we've produced. I'm definitely one of

the people who came at it loose—no sin, no taboos—but maybe we were too egalitarian. If you are trying to raise a child without guilt, you run the danger of producing a child without conscience."

It is, it turns out, difficult to have it both ways. One cannot be both Huck Finn and Aunt Polly, one cannot be both rebel and elder. Having unseated their parents from their thrones of moral certainty, many of this generation found it hard to settle themselves in the vacated chairs. And while I personally would argue that much has changed for the better as a result of the broad assault on sexual and social hypocrisy waged during those years, one of its unintended effects, along with a decline in "institutional loyalty" of all kinds, has been a widespread inabilty to take one's adult self seriously as a figure of authority, resulting in a condition of helplessness that earlier generations may well have felt but were less likely to admit to, or to act on. As one mother described it to me, "I wish there *were* a higher authority. It would be a lot easier for children."

In fact, observes Mary Lou Sunderworth, the director of the lower school at Friends' Seminary in Manhattan, "a lot of children don't feel anybody is in charge. There is a feeling of insecurity in many children that is addressed only by a paid psychiatrist."

Sunderworth's observation is confirmed by psychiatrist Sirgay Sanger, whose Early Care Center treats troubled children and their parents. "Where people don't have a religion," Sanger says, "I may be cited as the authority: 'You must behave. We must, too. Dr. Sanger wants all of us to behave.' For some parents it is church that provides that necessary ethical structure."

Still, Sanger adds, "It's possible to say to the child, 'You may think that Mommy and Daddy are the biggest people in the world, but in reality we are all part of a larger system. We obey a higher power, whether it's God or society. Doing what we tell you to do doesn't humiliate you, because we're not humiliated by what we must do.' Most parents don't know how to set limits without humiliation."

Not all parental equivocation can be traced to lack of backbone, however. The wisest of parents may always have known what was at stake in a given situation, and which misbehavior to take how seriously, but for most ordinary parents, the guidelines provided by religion or the perceived mores of an *apparently* homogeneous culture provided a much needed frame of reference. Not only have culture and religion changed in profound ways in the last quarter century, but our reading of the social "text"—as the deconstructionists might put it—has been subverted. "Fifty years ago," says writer Lore Segal, who speaks from the perspective of having lived in three different cultures, and describes her own grown children as "nonreligious, virtuous" people, "everybody knew what was right and what to do. Now you have to figure it out. Figure out what is decency, what is ethics, what is proper behavior. How do you handle something when tradition no longer tells you how?"

Modern parents tutored in psychology—or half-tutored, as is more frequently the case—find themselves pincered between alternative readings of ordinary events. They recognize that much of children's misbehavior (and that includes lying, stealing, and bashing one another) has far more to do with development than with morality, and they are loathe to stifle it. Which egregious incidents are evidence of moral warping, which of a predictable, transient stage? What should one ignore, and what take seriously? Obviously this can be carried to ludicrous extremes of indulgence, but the middle ground is fertile enough territory for parental indecision. Has Josh bashed Maria with his Ninja sword because he is an incipient gang leader or because it's six P.M., he is four years old, and he failed to take his nap? Or, more guilt-inducing, is it because both his parents leave for work at eight in the morning not to be seen again till seven, and he is furious about it and wants more of their attention?

"Psychology," observes Elizabeth Friar Williams, a San Francisco therapist and counselor at a Catholic boys' school, "has helped people to see things from more than one point of view, and therefore makes them less likely to accept an authoritarian position, or to take an authoritarian position themselves. They recognize that punishment is not necessarily the best way to deal with the tensions and problems that cause children's misbehavior and are generally more willing to consider another approach. The problem for a lot of parents is that they don't know what a useful substitute might be."

However confused contemporary parents may be about exercising their moral authority or interpreting their children's behavior, some needed perspective can be drawn from a consideration of how "unconfused" parents were once encouraged to go about it. In *Spare the Child: The Religious Roots of Punishment and the Psychological Impact of Physical Abuse,* Philip Greven describes the long history of corporal punishment of children in America and its explicit religious justification. Illuminated by scores of pitiless aphorisms drawn from the Bible ("Chasten thy son while there is hope and let not thy soul spare for its crying"; "The blueness of a wound cleanseth away evil: so do stripes the inward parts of the belly"), this tradition was based on the conviction that any challenge to parental authority was dangerous and sinful, to be rooted out in infancy lest it gain strength and lead to more calamitous resistance to the will of God. Thus Greven cites an admiring account of the child-rearing practices of Sarah Edwards, the wife of the famous eighteenth-century preacher Jonathan Edwards. By the standards of the day, Sarah Edwards's hand was light and seldom raised, but strictly in consequence of her having done her work early and well.

"Her system of discipline," wrote her grandson Sereno Dwight, "*was begun at a very early age,* and it was her rule to *resist the first,* as well as every subsequent exhibition of temper or disobedience in the child, *however young,* until its will was brought into submission to the will of its parents: wisely reflecting, that until a child will obey his parents, he can never be brought to obey God." (Emphasis added by Greven.)

That this philosophy was not simply theoretical is clear from Greven's next citation, of a letter from Sarah's daughter Esther, married by then to the Reverend Aaron Burr, president of Princeton University. Writing to a friend in 1754, two years before giving birth to the future vice-president (and eventual victor in America's most famous duel), the young mother made a confession of maternal discipline that blends earnest solicitude with shocking brutality. "I had almost forgot to tell you," she wrote, "that I have begun to govourn Sally. She has been

Whip'd once . . . and she knows the difference between a smile and a frown as well as I do. When she has done anything that she Surspects is wrong, will look with concern to see what Mama says, and if I only knit my brow she will cry till I smile, and *altho She is not quite Ten months old,* yet when she knows so much, I think tis time she should be taught." (Emphasis added.)

Breaking the will of the child through violence, Greven argues, was more than an inclination toward cruelty and dominance; it was perceived religious duty, and only rarely admitted of equivocation or doubt. The guiding principle was to root out intransigence, to drive out sin. "Foolishness is bound in the heart of a child; but the rod of correction shall drive it far from him," runs one of the Solomonic advisories quoted by Greven.

If it was commonly believed necessary, as one survivor of a turn-of-the-century apocalyptic sect described it, "to break a child's spirit" in order to insure his salvation, so be it. And it is this willingness to "break" the child as much as the physical brutality (against which we now have civil laws) that strikes most modern parents as an alien and abhorrent ambition. It bespeaks a refusal to see the child for his own sake or to imagine in him a capacity for reason—failures that mock the Christian notions of free will and the sanctity of the individual as well as the possibility of benign parental example. In this conception of goodness, achieved through brute force, virtue is yielded up as a sort of parboiled residue of the human soul, a virtue based not on the emulation of an admirable model and the refinement of a personal conscience, but on fear of the stick.

In *A Good Enough Parent,* Bruno Bettelheim touches

repeatedly on the issue of authority versus emulation in the development of conscience, including an entire chapter entitled "Why Punishment Doesn't Work," in which he reminds us that "Any punishment—physical or emotional—sets us against the person who inflicts it on us."

"The young child," he writes, "cannot distinguish between the morally good and the morally bad. He knows only what feels good and what doesn't, what he likes and dislikes. Thus, filial love will induce him to emulate his parent, whatever the nature of his parents' morals—he will identify with good as well as bad traits." And again: "A child is rarely convinced something is wrong simply because his parents say it is. It *becomes* wrong to him because he wishes to be loved by his parents, to be thought well of by them. Since the best way to be loved, in the short run, is to do what the parents approve, and in the long run, to become like them, he identifies with their values. This identification is thus the result of loving and admiring parents, not of being punished by them."

And finally: "We must at all times retain our conviction of [children's] inner goodness, acknowledging that it just takes a long time for our example to come to fruition, as it did in our own lives."

Long before I came upon Bettelheim's discussion of this barely perceptible process of internalization of parental values, it was described for me by Danya and Tamar Kraft-Stolar, two young sisters I interviewed about growing up without God. Raised as atheists by parents who were fiercely moral and politically active, they gradually became aware that other children sometimes linked their good behavior to religious proscriptions, while theirs was linked only to the standards set by their parents.

"She fought for what she believed in," Danya recalled in an essay about her mother, written as part of an application to high school a year after her mother's death. "She once made me miss my best friend's birthday party to go to a peace march in 1980."

"When I was little," said Danya, "I never associated any values with religion. I didn't know what religion was. It was enough that my parents told me what was right and wrong." Her younger sister echoed the experience. "I always thought it was enough that my parents said so. When I got a little older, and began to understand about religion, I might have felt, Where do you get the right or the authority to tell me what to do? But I never really felt it wasn't enough, that I needed more of a purpose to do something than because my parents told me to. Now," she said, "it's because I know what I'm supposed to do."

Though the process of internalizing one's parents' values seems relatively simple in retrospect, and especially when successful, for some children it is a process that asks too much. "In the past," says Dr. Sirgay Sanger, "it was sufficient to have a child adhere to the parents' religion. Now all parents want is that their child be happy and adjusted to the here and now. We want children to think for themselves." Though a less authoritarian expectation, it is also a more demanding one, comparable, observes Eileen Gillooly, to the greater expectations placed on a child by many aspects of modern life.

"It's a little bit like an open classroom, in which children are always supposed to be working independently, even though they may be desperate for more direction. When you raise a child without religion, you make a child internalize standards and expectations at a very early age—something I was never expected to do. It's hard enough for adults, who for the most part have had orthodox religious training. So I suppose I feel as guilty about not being able to give her an external authority as I would if I were to give her a religious training I didn't believe in myself."

Whatever it is that parents hope church attendance or Sunday school will insure—"a nice life," a habit of conscience, fewer opportunities to stray—the results of a survey of five thousand American schoolchildren, conducted for the Girl Scouts of the United States of America and published in 1990, suggest that its influence is real, but rather difficult to isolate. Based on an economic and racial cross section of children from grades four through twelve at 233 schools in forty-eight states, *The Beliefs and Moral Values of America's Children* examined both specific moral behavior and the ways in which children form their personal values. Children were asked whom they trusted, in whom they confided, who their heroes were, and what they worried about. It charted the changing moral concerns of children as they mature and the changing nature of the pressures and influences that work on them as they approach independence.

As a social document, it is both touching and disturbing—a reminder of how predictably history repeats itself despite our best intentions, of how fixed our limits tend to remain. Reading not unlike the results of a confidential poll of taxpayers (Do you always report your full income?) or of married couples (Have you ever engaged in sexual intercourse with a person other than your spouse?), the survey suggests that children's moral dilemmas come to resemble their parents' rather early life, and that it is not so much the spectacular sins that throw them off course as the routine pressures and banal seductions of everyday life. As they confess how they would act under a dozen theoretical circumstances posed by the interviewers—from cheating on a test at school to drinking at a party to "going all the way" with someone they love—these stand-ins for all our children display a range of opinion, character, and anxiety that in turn reflects the most common pressures of childhood: divided loyalties, the desire to be popular, the drive to succeed, the wish to be good. It is the difficulty of satisfying those competing aims that is most evident in the morally erratic behavior they report.

Asked whether they would glance at a neighbor's paper when taking an important test for which they had not prepared, for example, 12 percent of the children said outright that they would, ranging from a low of 5 percent for elementary school children to a high of 17 percent for high school students. Another 35 percent, however, more intent on preserving the illusion of their own honesty, perhaps, or conceivably more genuinely confused about what cheating means, said they would just "glance" at a neighbor's work "for ideas." Once again, there was a wide gap between younger and older children, 16 percent versus 48 percent.

There was less confusion about whether it was all right to take money from one's parents without permission in order to go out with friends. Only 5 percent of the children surveyed said they would take the money (with no appreciable difference by age), while 67 percent "would try to get permission first" and 26 percent said they would forgo the money. Reading this, I was reminded of a former college professor of mine who had confessed that his extreme scrupulousness about money matters—never pocketing the extra nickel mistakenly given in change, never forgetting to repay a borrowed dollar—was, in some sense, meant to balance out his inability to find so clear a path when it came to matters of love or friendship. And, indeed, when obliged to choose between loyalty to a friend and honesty, life quickly does become more complicated, especially among older children. "Some school property has been destroyed," one question begins. "Your best friend brags to you that he did it. The school principal asks if you know what happened. In this situation, you would probably . . . ?" Overall, 36 percent of the children in the survey said they would deny any knowledge of the vandalism, while 23 percent would deny knowing anything when asked but then leave a note; 24 percent said they would tell the truth; 17 percent said they did not know what they would do.

There were modest differences in how boys and girls would respond under the circumstances, the boys more inclined to stonewall, the girls more inclined to leave a note. The only other significant difference had to do, predictably, with age. Only 14 percent of the elementary school children would lie to the principal, whereas 41 percent of junior high school students and 53 percent of senior high school students would.

A series of questions about alcohol use, sexual behavior, abortion, and suicide that were asked only of junior and senior high school students, provoked a wide range of answers, indicating not simply a lack of agreement be-

tween the two age groups, but the volatility of the subjects, even hypothetically considered. Offered a drink at
a party with friends, for example, 52 percent of the junior
high group and 42 percent of senior high group would
refuse. Another 16 and 8 percent, respectively, would
"take the glass but [only] pretend to drink"; 10 and 9
percent would "drink but not feel good" about it; and
17 and 34 percent would "drink without worrying."

There was a comparable splintering of opinion when
it came to sexual activity. Asked how far they would be
willing to "go" on the third date with someone they like
"very much," roughly a quarter of junior and high students said they would not go beyond kissing, while 40
percent said they would go some middle distance beyond
kissing, and 18 percent of the younger group and 24 percent of the older group said they would go "far beyond."
A subsequent question addressed the "far beyond" issue
directly, asking whether the students would agree to sex
with a boyfriend or girlfriend with whom they were
"very much in love." Overall, some 39 percent said they
would, compared to 24 percent who said they would
insist on waiting for marriage, but the difference between
the two age groups was considerable: while 47 percent
of the high school kids said they would have sex, only
27 percent of the junior high group said they would. More
striking, and less surprising, given the consequences, was
the gap between the sexes, with 54 percent of the boys
saying yes compared to 22 percent of the girls. Among
the girls, the most popular response was "insist on waiting till marriage" (30 percent), followed by the tempor-
izing "refuse to have sex for now" (26 percent) and the
anxious "try to hold off if you can" (22 percent).

Two questions on the highly emotional subject of abortion were posed, but both appeared to have been framed in such a way as to limit the students' need to admit to the possibility of having a personal stake in their answers. Thus the first asked not what a girl would do if she were pregnant, or what a boy would do if his girlfriend were pregnant, but rather what kind of advice either would give to a friend grappling with the question. Even so, it drew the highest percentage of "don't know" responses in the entire survey, 32 percent, suggesting that for teenagers, just as for adults, this remains a terribly difficult issue. While a slightly higher proportion, 36 percent, would tell the friend to have the baby and keep it, only 12 percent said they would recommend an abortion outright; another 21 percent would recommend having the baby and giving it up for adoption.

By contrast, the second-highest consensus in the "moral decisions" part of the survey came in response to a question asking who should have the final say in deciding whether a girl is to have an abortion. Despite the fact that only 12 percent of the students surveyed said they would actually recommend an abortion to a friend, 70 percent said they believed the girl herself should have the final say, compared to 13 percent who said it should be the parents and 17 percent who were unsure. For the most part, agreement on this issue cut across age, gender, race, income, academic standing, religious affiliation, and church attendance. Just one question elicited a greater consensus, 86 percent disagreeing with the statement "Suicide is all right because a person has the right to do whatever he wants with himself." (Interestingly, those most inclined to agree with the statement were from families receiving food stamps or with an unemployed adult in the home, while those who were most undecided on the issue were from households with incomes greater than $40,000 a year.)

The apparent contradiction between the high regard for life expressed in the antisuicide position and the more permissive standard applied in cases of abortion may reflect an underestimation of teenagers' grasp of death's finality—generally considered not all that certain—as well as their gift for the sort of ethical calculus adults resort to to measure the rights of a fetus against the long-term prospects of a young woman's life and independence.

What is most significant in the context of this discussion, however, is what the authors of the report term "the questionable role of religion" as a moral influence. Some 82 percent of the children surveyed claim to believe in God, 77 percent describe themselves as members of one religious denomination or another, and 57 percent say they attend church or synagogue at least once a week. When asked how they went about deciding "what was right or wrong in a situation," however, only 16 percent said they would "Do as Scripture says," an approach the report's authors term "theistic," and which they contrast with four other designated "moral compasses" by which children explain their moral reasoning: "expressivist" ("It makes me happy," 18 percent); "utilitarian" ("To get ahead," 10 percent); "civic humanist" ("Best for everyone," 23 percent) and "conventionalist" ("Follow the advice of an adult," 21 percent).

Similarly, though 34 percent of the children surveyed answered yes to the question "Has there ever been a minister, priest, or rabbi who had been an important influence in your life?" only 3 percent said they would consult a religious leader for advice when uncertain "what the right thing is to do," and only 2 percent would turn to God for answers. In comparison, some 64 percent would look to a parent and 43 percent would talk to a friend of the same age, with younger children being more inclined to the former, junior and senior high school students more inclined to the latter. While it is hardly surprising that elementary school children would not be trotting down to the minister's house for a chat, it appears not to be a temptation that increases with greater mobility and independence.

Yet just as one is about to dismiss the influence of organized religion on young people altogether, a series of cross-tabulations is offered to suggest that, even among those children "whose moral assumptions are *not* religiously oriented," regular church attendance does indeed have a modest positive effect on moral behavior, making such children "less . . . willing to cheat, lie or steal, drink alcohol underage, or be libertarian in their decisions about their sexual behavior." Given that equal or greater statistical differences turn up between children of different ages, or between children reasoning from "expressivist" or "civic humanist" positions, it is a necessarily limited endorsement of the power of churchgoing to affect behavior.

Somewhat more potent, I would argue, is the example of the parents who arranged for thir children's regular attendance in the first place. However varied children's moral compasses, or inconsistent their interpretations of given moral issues, the clear evidence of the survey is that they remain linked by their reliance on, and confidence in, their parents and families. When asked which "special adults in your life really care about you," 95 percent of the children surveyed listed parents first. What parents do, how they themselves behave, and what they expect of their children remain the critical factors in the formation of moral perspective, whether the parent's personal convictions are expressed in weekly church attendance—or in dragging one's child to a peace march when she would rather go to a friend's birthday party.

What I take to be most revelatory about the survey in the long run, however, is what it discloses about a far-reaching but rarely remarked shift in American religiosity, in which moral values have been separated from the traditional theism on which they are based like an egg white from its golden yolk. So that even as the overwhelming majority of Americans continue to describe themselves as religious, and their children echo the claim, the ethical wellspring for most is no longer the triangular ideal of traditional theology, in which one's goodness and one's connection to one's neighbor derive from a relationship to God, but the quite different rubrics of civic humanist ("Best for everyone") or conventionalist ("Follow the advice of an adult"). In other words, a set of moral standards that derive from a particular religious conviction while no longer depending on it.

It is tempting to describe this shift in the metaphysical bedrock as further evidence of what many have begun to speak of as "postmodern religion"—an imprecise, if fervently espoused, creed that permits one to believe pretty much whatever one likes without being obliged to surrender the claim of membership in one or another of the standard traditions. Several of the parents I talked to spoke dismissively, for example, of Unitarianism as the "creedless creed," or of Unitarians as the "committed uncommitted." In fact, Unitarians, who profess an optional *theos,* have simply proclaimed openly what large portions of the mainstream churches practice unacknowledged—a morality based no longer on the fear of God's wrath or the threat of eternal punishment but on the recognition of humanity's shared obligations. "To worry about whether or not there is a God, or whether there is an 'up there' or a 'down there' seems irrelevant," said Penny Coleman, one of many nonreligious parents for whom a social conscience is the critical measure of morality. "The important thing is to deal with issues of homelessness, racism, human justice, and to teach your children how to deal with them in turn."

The gradual substitution of civic humanism, or even the dread "secular humanism," for the theistic absolutism espoused by so many rival claimants may be the "slippery slope" complained of by conservatives, but for many people it represents a much-needed broadening of the moral canvas and a release from the narrow and competing claims of denominational certitude. Given this country's extraordinary religious pluralism, such a move toward a common, less explicitly theistic, ground has long been inevitable. Nevertheless, for a people rooted in a tradition of religious "exceptionalism"—what professor William Dean has described in the journal *Religion and American Culture* as America's idea of itself as "religiously superior" to other nations—it is an unsettling shift indeed.

Whatever the current reality, this image of ourselves as

a people blessed and apart continues, as Gary Wills argues in *Under God,* to exert a profound influence on our national political life. "Religion has always been at the center of our major political crises, which are always moral crises," Wills observes. And rarely is the particular vision of American exceptionalism on bolder display than in time of war.

"Religion is such an essential ingredient of the American character," UCLA history professor Robert Dallek told a reporter for the *New York Times* shortly after the start of the war with Iraq, "that when you get into a war, as during times of peace, Americans want to have a sort of moral enterprise, moral imperative, which stands at the center of what they do."

Other countries may go to war for venal purposes; America goes to war against monsters, for the little guy, to make the world "safe for democracy"—or, as one reporter suggested early in the Gulf crisis, to make it "safe for feudalism." And indeed, a month into the war, when news came that hundreds of Iraqi civilians had been killed in a single bombing raid—a raid whose purpose was fiercely debated here and abroad—many Americans would react to the news by insisting on our inability to have a hand in something so grisly. It was not enough to say it was awful, as many genuinely felt, or to concede the certain, but heretofore little remarked, inevitability of civilian deaths in any city under attack, however surgical. What was necessary to a great many Americans was to say that we just don't do that sort of thing, period. "I'm sure it was an accidental bombing," one man was quoted as saying in the *New York Times*. "I don't think our government is into civilian bombing." "I believe," said another, "that the American people have an appreciation for human life, and we're trying to fight this war with as little loss of life as possible."

Such expressions of faith in our superior virtue may be shortsighted or wishful, but to the degree that they arise out of an inherited cultural self-image and an admirable longing to in fact *be* good, I do not think they are especially hypocritical. Rather, they reflect a widespread conviction that the American tradition embodies the best and the purest political ideals—that we are, indeed, a nation "under God," and one privy to His truest aims. We are good, this faith holds, because we are a believing people, and because we are a believing people, our motives will be consistently correct. It is, of course, the reading virtually all peoples have insisted on for themselves throughout history. It is a conceit most easily sustained when the gods of the combatants are also rivals, but that has never been essential. "Every attack we carry out against the Iraqis," a Saudi squadron commander was quoted as saying in the *New York Times,* "is carried out in the name of Mohammed." And the French had Joan of Arc.

"I tell my kids," says Nancy Gallin, "how American soldiers during World War I would find German soldiers dead at the end of a battle and see on their helmets 'God Is with You,' and how shocked they were by it. The point is, everybody does it. Which is why the most dangerous thing on the planet is the idea of *them* and *us*. God is always on *our* side."

As if to reinforce the image of ourselves as a "people of God," it is significant that we have kept steady before us as the appropriate contrast not the score of democratic Western nations that derive their social policies from the

same Judeo-Christian ideals we espouse but the anti-
thetical, and suddenly dated, image of "godless com-
munism," the system whose every motive we have held
to be self-interested and malign.

In the December 1989 issue of the *Atlantic Monthly,*
Glenn Tinder, a professor of political science at the University of Massachusetts, takes up the question of whether
political morality can be sustained outside a specifically
religious framework. In his essay "Can We Be Good
Without God; The Political Meaning of Christianity,"
Tinder argues, thoughtfully and at some length, that political morality cannot be sustained outside a specifically
religious framework, for without the Judeo-Christian
concept of the "exalted individual" the state cannot be
relied upon to stay its hand, and all notions of equality
and responsibility evaporate. "It is hardly too much to
say," Tinder writes, "that the idea of the exalted individual is the spiritual center of Western politics. Although
this idea is often forgotten and betrayed, were it erased
from our minds our politics would probably become altogether what it is at present only in part—an affair of
expediency and self-interest."

As Tinder acknowledges early on, the most powerful
counter to his position is the example of the Enlightenment, which, many people would argue, did more to
advance the dignity and rights of the individual than any
monarch ruling by divine right, or any representative of
official religion. "Locke and Jefferson, it will be asserted,
not Jesus and Paul, created our moral universe," he writes,
and he concedes that the Enlightenment "has sometimes
played a constructive role. It has translated certain Christian values into secular terms and, in an age becoming

increasingly secular, has given them political force. It is doubtful, however, that it could have created those values or that it can provide them with adequate metaphysical foundations."

That, finally, is Tinder's ultimate position—that however idealistic or loving the individual proponents of secular humanism, and despite the fact that "the Enlightenment carried into action political ideals that Christians, in contravention of their own basic faith, often shamefully neglected or denied," rational regard for one's fellow men and women is insufficient by itself to sustain public morality. The "illogic" of morality absent a God will eventually catch up with the most high-minded of creatures.

This is so, Tinder argues, even though "we all know many people who do not believe in God and yet are decent and admirable," and despite the fact that "Western societies, as highly secularized as they are, retain many humane features."

"Not even tacitly," he writes, "has our sole governing maxim become the one Dostoyevski thought was bound to follow the denial of the God-man: 'Everything is permitted.' This may be, however, because customs and habits formed during Christian ages keep people from professing and acting on such a maxim even though it would be logical to do so. If that is the case," he concludes, "our position is precarious, for good customs and habits need spiritual grounds, and if those are lacking, they will gradually, or perhaps suddenly in some crisis, crumble."

What so troubles Tinder at the "macro" level of political morality is what might be thought to trouble parents on a more intimate scale—in theory, at any rate.

"Can children be good without God?" has the sound of a serious "big" question, particularly, one would think, to parents who have chosen to go it alone after childhoods spent within the religious fold. Yet, for most parents I talked to, believers as well as nonbelievers, it was a question without much real urgency. With few exceptions—the most vivid being that of a father struggling to retain belief because "the only thing that gives human flesh any dignity is that Christ assumed it"—morality was seen as a *human* issue, not a theological one, "being good" an outgrowth of acquired empathy and conscience, not religious belief or religious guilt.

"I don't think there is a God who is waiting to punish you if you are not good," said Jenny Allen. "I was never motivated by that idea and would hope that Halley never would be, either."

"As a psychologist," says Yona Rothwax, whose own two children had no exposure to religion when they were growing up, "I felt absolutely sure that the moral development would take care of itself. There is no question in my mind that a child raised in a religious home is no more moral or ethical. Now that I have rediscovered Judaism for myself, I feel it adds a dimension to one's life that I regret not giving my kids, but I don't think it has anything to do with whether they are good people or not."

Even among the actively religious, theological references were oddly absent. Believing parents spoke more of "moral guidance," "moral grounding," "family values," "judgment," and "help in decision making" than they did of an unchanging, unshaded moral code or an omniscient Enforcer.

"My children don't get God as a reason to behave from

me," said Sally Shea, a practicing Catholic who has raised
her children in a church greatly changed since she was a
child, a church in which the rite of "confession" has been
supplanted by the rite of "reconciliation," and the ancient
threat of hell is barely mentioned at all. "I tell them, 'You
know what's right and what's wrong. If you want to call
it a sin, you can.' "

Among Catholics of my generation—and for most of
the preceding nineteen centuries as well—eternal dam-
nation was the big stick meant to insure both moral conformity and institutional loyalty. The paths to hell were
many and sweetly paved, we were told, its fires stoked
with an inexhaustible supply of sinners. These days,
though the inferno has yet to be officially extinguished,
"It is not," as one parish priest carefully put it, "mentioned nearly so much." And not only by Catholics. "Hell
has disappeared and no one noticed," observed Protestant
theologian Martin E. Marty in a 1991 piece in *U.S. News
and World Report* that purported to explore a renewed
theological interest in the subject. Led by theologians and
a generally rationalist clergy, mainstream Protestants have
abandoned hell in droves, while the fire and brimstone
of evangelical tradition has in most churches cooled to
Jacuzzi temperatures. "My congregation would be
stunned to hear a sermon on hell," a Methodist minister
from Washington, D.C., told the newsmagazine, which
added that "Kenneth S. Kantzer, a former editor of the
evangelical magazine *Christianity Today,* confessed . . .
that he hadn't preached a sermon on hell in more than
three decades." These are sensible enough adaptations to
the fact that only 60 percent of the population continues
to believe in hell anyway, and then mainly for other peo-

ple: only 4 percent of those who say there is a hell expect to find out for themselves if they are right, according to *U.S. News* figures.

Just how great a change has taken place became clear to me a couple of years ago in the course of a conversation with my sister Ginny and her two older children. Ginny herself does not believe in a geographic hell, but rather in something akin to a final "alienation" from God, and it was clear from the subsequent discussion that the question of hell has not dominated her children's late-night thoughts the way they did mine. Her daughter Natalie, who was then eleven, was describing some of her ideas about God and religion for me, and after explaining what sin meant to her—an admirably simple "something bad that you do, against what God wants you to do"—she arrived at the subject of an earned afterlife. "If you're good, you go to heaven," she announced with an inflection appropriate to describing a trip to Disneyland, "and if you're bad, you go to hell." She was about to go on to some other point when her brother Evan, who was seven at the time, interrupted. "There's no such thing as hell," he insisted, "not even if you're the Night Stalker!"

Running through most discussions of morality and ethics are the related themes of altruism and self-sacrifice, as if decency were largely a consequence of self-denial, and therefore extraordinarily difficult to insure. In fact, observes Dan Menaker, the father of two young children, while "the ethical and moral principles espoused by most religions are good for the most part, and worth following, I would argue it is for the opposite of reasons usually put forward: they represent enlightened self-interest. The cardinal tenet of Christianity is one of the most self-interested of principles. Because if everybody 'did unto others,' we would all benefit enormously. I think it is a worthy principle and it sets up a useful goal for human society and human relations. I also think, psychologically, that to be what society and religion call 'a bad person' makes one's life terribly hard."

What has occurred, in fact, in a process both natural and inevitable, is that the religious values Glenn Tinder deems to be at the root of morality have long since been converted into secular values that are subscribed to in equal measure by those who practice a religion and those who do not, by those who adhere to them in real life and those who fail to. "Whether people know it or not, think about it or not," says Jan Miller, an administrator in a nonreligious private school, "we live in a Judeo-Christian culture. The tradition permeates our thinking. However they may behave on a given issue, Americans are steeped in the idea of the sanctity of the individual. The whole notion of health and happiness as an individual right— we haven't lost the Judeo-Christian code, we've secular-ized it into our laws."

Like a handful of parents I talked to, Miller speaks from the perspective of someone who has lived on both sides of the religious question. Raised in a secular household by atheist parents, she, in turn, raised her son without belief, only to come to faith and the tradition of her Episcopalian grandparents in her mid-thirties. She has no illusions about organized religion as a guarantor of mo-rality. "My son is one of the most moral people I know," she says; but she argues forcefully in favor of the Western ideals that originated in the Judeo-Christian tradition. "There is a difference," she says, and cites as example her twenty-year-old son's recent experience as a volunteer with Mother Teresa in India. Like most Westerners, he was stunned by the fatalistic acceptance of misery he encountered in the streets. " 'People just step over bodies and say it's as it should be,' " his mother quotes him reporting in astonishment. " 'It's their karma, they must have done something terrible to deserve this.' "

"Here," Miller argues, where the rising tide of homeless and an increasing objectification of the poor as a class apart make comparison with life along the Ganges unavoidable, "we at least struggle with it. When you pass a homeless person on the street, do you say to your child, 'It doesn't matter, he's lower than dung?' No, you say, 'This is a terrible thing, no one should live this way, we must do more for people even if I can't personally give money to every person I see.' You say, 'That's a human being, with hopes and aspirations like our own.' And you struggle with it."

Nancy Gallin made much the same point from the perspective of an atheist who claims that "the Enlightenment is my religion." She and her husband, Richard, she said, had taken two of their eight children to a concert in honor of the fiftieth anniversary of the Battle of Britain. "There was all this stirring music meant to evoke the heroic stand of the English against Hitler, and we were all very moved. I found myself saying to Richard the next morning, 'You know, that was the last time the good guys were on the right side. It wasn't confusing, we knew what was right and what was wrong.' And a big part of it had to do with what Churchill said in a recording they played during the evening from a speech he made at the time, something about 'the very survival of Christian civilization' being at stake. And I found that as a 'non-Christian,' and an atheist, I wasn't offended at all, because I felt I knew what he meant and that I agreed with him. He meant a whole tradition of Western values that I share, and that I think *are* better than other value systems. There is something about those values that stirs the soul."

To a great extent, what we are talking about is a process of moral evolution that stretches from the time of Abraham (if not earlier) to the present, continually incorporating new notions of morality to accommodate changing visions of what we mean by "good." Certainly the Judeo-Christian tradition by which we claim to live today is not the Judeo-Christian tradition of medieval Europe, nor of the nineteenth century; rather, it is one revision in a succession of revisions of that tradition. Even to speak of the tradition as *Judeo-Christian* is by definition to record one of its most recent updatings, in which the officially espoused anti-Semitism of the Christian world has given way to a belated acknowledgement of the debt Christianity owes its parent faith. In contrast to our religious forefathers (foremothers, one does well to remember, did not count), we no longer chop off people's heads in the name of God, nor do we burn them at the stake to save their souls; we do not take schizophrenia for demonic possession, nor do we baptize the heathen at the point of a sword. And however much they resemble our own prior excesses, we are collectively shocked by what we judge to be the religious excesses of other creeds—most conspicuously, at present, those of Islam. The fact is that morality too has its fashions, and while the most ancient biblical proscriptions against violence to one's neighbor's life and property have long since been incorporated into civil law, the business of deciding what is moral behavior in a given society remains conspicuously unfinished.

Practices that were morally acceptable to the majority of our ancestors—slavery, for instance, followed by a century of legally enforced segregation—are now seen by most people as morally indefensible, while social arrangements long condemned as immoral—couples living together without benefit of marriage, divorce, homosexual unions—are increasingly accepted, in some cases to the extent of enjoying both the protection of law and the practical (if less often the official) endorsement of the more liberal religious groups. Other subjects, meanwhile, continue to generate furious moral controversy—with ethical issues such as abortion and medically assisted suicide, the waging of war, and the fair distribution of wealth evoking equally fervent moral arguments from every side.

For all this ongoing conflict, most discussions of morality presuppose, nevertheless, some irreducible principle of moral formulation that has man at its center. In traditional Judeo-Christian theology, humans take their sacredness, their inviolability, and their worth from the God who made them and in whose image they were wrought. Their value is thus derivative but singular, their position at the pinnacle of living things unassailable. It is, indeed, this exaltation of the human because of its link to the divine that has elevated the rhetoric and the ideals of Western civilization to the heights we take to be unparalleled. In the view of a newly emergent generation of moralists, however, this same tradition is to blame for an equally unparalleled record of ruination in the form of man's historic misuse of the earth and violence against its nonhuman inhabitants.

Under this new dispensation (sometimes referred to as "deep ecology" or a "theology of nature") man's inhumanity to man no longer stands as the truest measure of his indecency, but must share equal billing with environmental sins past and present—from the clearing of the rain forests and the depletion of the ozone layer to the slaughter of the buffalo and the sperm whale, to the testing of vaccines on monkeys, the suffocation of dolphins in tuna nets, and veal piccata for dinner.

Thus is the divine entitlement of man reduced to the charge of "speciesism," the unwarranted ranking of inherently equal claimants by the beasts at the top of the heap—us. Defined by one animal liberationist as "the presumption that humans are superior to other sentient creatures," speciesism is not simply the latest of a series of "isms" in need of moral and political correctives, but a leap of ideology that profoundly undermines many of our long-held notions as to the meaning of "human." It is not merely a plausible and overdue demand for greater regard for our common nest but a determination that nest and householder are equal. In "deep ecology" the once respectable notion of stewardship is discarded, and replaced with the even-stephency of the time-share.

What is of significance in this discussion is the innate appeal of such ethical arguments to children. As the natural allies of dolphins, bunny rabbits, newborn calves, and other creatures that mirror their own particular helplessness, children are instinctive "antispeciesists." (Not for nothing has Saint Francis been among the most popular of children's saints—and not for nothing has the

Church had the sense to play up the animals and play down the naked-in-the-streets part of the story.) Not only are they drawn to identify with "nonsentient" creatures as mute versions of themselves; most have no experience of animals save as adorable pets or equally adorable fantasy companions, anthropomorphized into absolute equality. Thus they conceive of animals neither as plausible threats nor as part of the historic food chain but as inviolate creatures in their own right. Every pig is Wilbur, every deer Bambi, every elephant Babar.

While it can be said that today's parents underwent similar affectionate identification with animals when they were children—only to emerge, most of us, as unregenerate speciesists—in fact, there was nothing in our childhoods to compare with the emphasis on the environment and the rights of animals that envelops children today, nor with the sectarian edginess that fuels the many arbiters of political correctness.

A small example. When I was growing up, every classroom in my Catholic grammar school displayed a small cardboard box with a grainy photograph of a Chinese child on the side. It was a bank into which we were encouraged to drop our extra coins, and for every five dollars we collected, we were able, as we said with antedeluvian innocence, to "buy a pagan baby." As I recall the process, the class would vote whether it wanted to buy a boy or a girl, would offer a name for baptism and mail the cash to something called the Holy Childhood Association (every diocese had one). In retrospect, I assume that the funds thus raised went to salvage the thousands of postwar Chinese (and later Korean) orphans sheltered and educated for nothing more (or less) than the

price of Christian baptism—a form of religious imperi-
alism, surely, but one based, at least, on a conviction that
the human soul was meant to be redeemed and the human
body fed and clothed. Salvation was the conscious ob-
jective, and every human was deemed equally worthy of
being saved. Indeed, I can still recall the fervor with which
we dwelled on those lucky souls snatched from the jaws
of limbo by our pennies.

The moral basis of missionary activity has, of course,
undergone considerable refining since (so much so, in
fact, that the Pope has had to remind the Catholic faithful
that, ecumenism or no, there are souls still to be saved
out there). Not only would it be grotesquely incorrect
politically to encourage one's children to "buy a pagan
baby" as from an evangelic gift catalog, but one is increasingly obliged, when contemplating pledging one's
pennies, to sort out a tangle of social and political griev-
ances claiming moral legitimacy. It all depends on one's
moral-political leanings, and the latest news bulletins.
Thus I was struck one day by an innovative application
of the rescue impulse in an Episcopalian Sunday school
class I visited. The children were pooling their pennies
to adopt, not some earthquake-orphaned child thousands
of miles distant, or a future leader of the Shining Path
(reminiscing about pagan babies one evening during the
Vietnam War, the president of my Catholic college said,
"Ah yes, I remember. I adopted Ho Chi Minh.") but an
endangered blue whale. The whale in question was already named and certified by the sponsoring environmental group, and was, regardless of how far gone some
religious environmentalists might be, in no need of baptizing. This, it struck me, was the perfect, and politically
correct, segue—from pagan baby to baby whale.

It helps, as Jan Miller wisely points out, "to take the long view" of such shifts in moral temper. Historically, she says, "there have always been these swings of awareness, and they are necessary and useful." We have gone too far in our abuse of the earth and our assertions of our own dominance, making such corrective posturing inevitable.

Whether our children will prove any better or worse than their parents or previous generations trailing backward into history is probably a matter beyond demonstrating. But I think an argument can be made that their understanding of good and bad will be different from ours, in ways subtle and profound. Our moral obligations as children were by definition minor and personal: we were told we had responsibility for our own souls—for not lying, cheating, stealing toys from the five-and-dime. We have told our children that their moral burden is the world itself: to insure peace, to guarantee justice, to free the oppressed and redeem the bleeding earth. We should not be surprised if their moral imaginations assume a global and apocalyptic cast.

It is, indeed, difficult to be good, as it always has been. "The great challenge in life," as Dan Menaker put it, "is to figure these things out. Most daily conflicts are very complicated. They are not black and white, and to work them out is not always easy. Shakespeare was a royalist and many of the things he believed are anathematic to me. But the cultural aim of a just and humane society is something he clearly aspired to. In the same sense, every novel is a utopia, and even the bleakest work contains a glimpse of the way things might be, if people could only be good."

Chapter 4

TRADITION AND CULTURE

"I do wish my kids had some understanding of religious culture. There is a black hole in their educations. They went to see *The Last Temptation of Christ* and came back saying, 'What a great story!' "

—Marian Taylor

Easter appears on the calendar ten days into spring this year (1991) as I write; the first night of Passover falls between Good Friday's passion and Easter morning's Hosannas. In the supermarket line an old woman complains that the price of eggs has shot up, and the papers are full of ads for kosher wines and off-the-shoulder "Easter dresses," recipes for hot cross buns and matzoh ball soup, lists of churches offering oratorios and restaurants offering seders. Schools are variously on or about to begin their spring or Easter break, the airlines are offering spring discounts and the major leagues are in spring training (Opening Day comes eight days after Easter this year, and like all major feasts, it is reverently capitalized). An ad for a long-running revue spoofing Catholic nuns cannot resist the ecumenical pun: "DON'T PASSOVER NUNSENSE," it implores, while one for a liquor store asks, "Why is this Passover similar to other Passovers?" (Answer: because the store is having its annual Passover sale.)

But the representational overload of the season is most perfectly captured by a newspaper review of Radio City

Music Hall's "Easter Show," a pastiche of high-kicking and convoluted symbolism that is to religion what the Super Bowl half-time is to patriotism, a "ninety-minute entertainment," in the reviewer's words, that unfolds "with a minimum of transitional clunk" from "light-hearted compilation of Easter-related iconography" into "giddy salute to spring."

"One reason it works so well," the reviewer goes on to say, "is that its solemn moments come at the beginning. 'The Glory of Easter' prologue . . . presents a ceremonial procession in a spectacular Gothic cathedral set-ting . . . [that] matches one's most extravagant fantasies of Vatican pomp and ceremony while remaining vague about the religious meaning of it all."

As a description of the contemporary chasm between religious symbolism and religious content, the last quoted observation could hardly be improved on. For sheer sym-bolic confusion, surely nothing in the yearly calendar compares with the competing rites of spring. In the season of carnal and spiritual rebirth, sacred and profane mean-ings overlap, Judeo-Christian and pagan traditions com-bine, the most solemn and raucous of festivals are juxtaposed, and it seems less and less possible, less and less *necessary*, to comprehend any of it. Carnival precedes Lent, which is prelude, for many, not to the Resurrection but to Fort Lauderdale. The complex ancillary symbolism of the Christian Easter, meanwhile, is lifted from a mul-titude of sources, from the seder table, with its (unco-lored) hard-boiled eggs, lamb bone, and ritual wine, to pagan celebrations of the vernal equinox that emphasize the reawakening and rebirth of the earth—conceptions of renewal as dissimilar as Handel's *Messiah* and Stravinsky's *The Rite of Spring*.

"Easter is not about bunnies and bonnets," grumbles
a Catholic archbishop, but it is a complaint made to the
wind. Easter cohabits a seasonal feast and is thus invo-
luntarily about many things, including bunnies and bonnets—along with more transcendent (but far from
exclusively Christian) big ideas like resurrection. The
very name "Easter"—attachable these days like some generic tag to any product that can be flogged in the
spring—is itself borrowed, like the seemingly pious tradition of hot cross buns, from the thoroughly pagan Sax-
ons, whose name it was for their goddess of light. The
annually changing dates of Easter and Passover, in turn,
are based on lunar calculations first worked out to set the
dates of still more ancient festivals commemorating the
death and resurrection of the Near Eastern god-king Tam-
muz, or Dumuzi, as he was called in Sumerian.

But enough is enough. No theater audience wants to
be informed of every dress rehearsal slip-up or be made
to watch the actors apply their makeup before the curtain
rises. Just so, the churchgoer caught up in the moment
does not need his symbols parsed into their most primitive components, his one true thing reduced to an anthropologist's footnote. Religious ritual, along with the
language of religion and its sacred symbols, has, in fact,
only partly to do with the literal truth of the image presented. It has to do as well with emotional evocation,
with a reimagining of signal events, and with a delicate
aesthetic reconstruction of some commonly held idea that
is not rational but felt. It is meant not to help one be good
but to *feel;* to feel connected to one's fellow man or a part
of some great thing, to be uplifted and transported—to
move outside one's self for a time. To that extent, the
experience of ritual is not limited to the believer, but can

be appropriated and appreciated at some level by the non-believer or the nonparticipant as well, can be "read" by the initiate and the uninitiated to similar transcendent purpose. The heathen and the true believer are equally vulnerable to the soar of a cathedral nave or a Magnificat sung a cappella. It is a matter of temperament as much as of faith. The materials of religious ritual, after all, are all man-made, cousins to the profane customs of ordinary life. "I love ritual," one woman I interviewed said cheerfully, though she had not set foot inside a church in thirty years save as wedding guest or mourner. "I love all the incense, the hymns. I'm wild about hymns."

It is, when done right, a great show, capable of overcoming one's deepest reservations, one's most self-protective defenses. "It's not Bach," one reluctant templegoer confessed a year or two after he'd begun attending occasional holiday services, "but I find it grows on you." As, of course, it is meant to.

Religious holidays that celebrate joy, meanwhile—the birth of a baby, the triumph of life over death, a people's escape into freedom—have a psychological and emotional resonance that transcends indoctrination in some specific theological system. They too can be "read" by a wide audience for their universal messages, and not just metaphorically.

And yet . . . For all that a catholicity of symbolism can be argued, true comprehension depends to some degree on an insider's knowledge. When my friend Nancy, trying to describe a scabrous virus that has raced through the nursery school our children attended, says to me, "It's like something out of the Bible," I know exactly what she means and that she and I share a culture that transcends her urban atheist (though bar mitzvahed) childhood and my suburban Catholic one. When my own daughter, theoretically heir to the same tradition, spies a pair of Saint Christopher statues on the dashboard of a taxicab and says, "Oh, look—chessmen!" I worry that she and I do not.

It is not so much that she cannot identify this debunked saint of my childhood, but that she has no inkling of a world in which the miraculous and the inexplicable play a role, nor of their attendant possibilities of intercession and improbable rescue. My childhood was imaginatively peopled with a saint for every contingency—Saint Christopher for journeys, Saint Anthony to find lost bracelets (in particular, and daily, my aunt's pocketbook), Saint Joseph to watch over our large family—as well as my own personal guardian angel, who always disappointed me by not making himself visible. My daughter's experience of miracles, by contrast, is limited to movies that combine traditional Christian symbols with secular pieties to produce something generally called "uplifting." *E.T.* is perhaps the most grandiose of these hokum spiritual feasts, though *Field of Dreams* cannot be far behind, and there are innumerable runners-up. A couple of seasons ago, I was forced to atone for never having viewed *Miracle on Thirty-fourth Street* from start to finish by watching the last half-hour of something called *One Magic Christmas*. In this instance, a mother who lacks the proper Christmas spirit is put through hell—her husband is shot and killed, her children kidnapped and driven into a river, presumed drowned—in the service of learning that Christmas matters. Along the way, her children are rescued from the icy river by a guardian angel in a fedora and her daughter comes to believe that her father can be restored to life by the agency of this same angel, named Gideon. When she asks this small favor, Gideon tells her he hasn't the power, but Santa Claus might. He thereupon whisks her to the North Pole, where Santa and Mrs. Claus bear a sharp resemblance to the *I Remember Mama* family, and where the elves in his workshop turn out to be the recently dead—content to replenish the world's supply of dolls, train sets, and Nintendo games for all eternity, one supposes. Heaven can wait.

The popularity of such pseudoreligious entertainments suggests unsatisfied longings for magical happy endings, for extraordinary and nonrational resolutions of life's difficulties—the very things religion once supplied with absolute assurance. In a world where paintings weep, statues bleed, and the sun spins blindingly in the sky, all things *are* possible. "Don't you worry that life becomes too *literal* without religion?" a friend who has no children of his own asked me one day, and indeed he had a point. Like art and music, religion gives voice to the inexpressible, shape and color to the unseen. However relaxed parents might be about going it alone metaphysically or morally, few I spoke to were sanguine about what they perceived as the emotional and cultural loss to their children of being raised without religion's shaping and celebratory power, without its stories and its poetry, without its web of symbols, and its magic. For some, it was primarily a sense of aesthetic deprivation, for others, a break in cultural continuity or a forced acknowledgment of how deeply the absence of faith cuts in daily life. "Not only can you not understand ritual, but you can't begin to understand most of your own cultural heritage, your own artistic

heritage, without some grounding in religion," said Katharine Bouton. "You can understand why Jews send their
kids to Hebrew school," said Penny Coleman. "Where
else are they going to find out about Jewish culture? Certainly not walking through the Metropolitan Museum."

For others, it was the nagging sense that, however
flawed, religion captured the ineffable and held a light to
it. Without its conceits of ritual and symbolism, the in-
substantial certainties we all privately harbor are in danger
of going unexpressed and unshared. Even among those
actively opposed to religion, there was agreement that
one cannot begin to comprehend history without knowing the part religion and religious faith have played in
human affairs.

It is one thing to give up the institution of religion,
quite another to jettison its sensory joys or its power to
anchor the individual in time and place. How much is a
May procession honoring the Virgin Mary worth in a
culture so bereft of reverence and community feeling as
the present? How much a creche on the hall table, a me-
zuzah by the front door, a church wedding, a baptism, a
bris? If one does not provide one's child with a tried and
true talisman—a cross, a rosary, a Jewish star to wear on
a chain—will one live to regret the child's embrace of a
crystal twenty years hence?

Since "losing" my faith many years ago, I cannot say,
as many others do, that I have envied anyone his certainty
of belief, but I have often envied the unconflicted use of
ritual that faith would permit—most particularly, the sort
of christening that Catholics and High Episcopalians specialize in and which in our house was rivaled only by the
closely overlapping sequence of First Communion, Con-

firmation, and big-sister-joins-the-convent parties. Never mind that I find the idea of original sin shocking—one of my still-believing sisters finds it senseless—or that I have no intention of raising my child a Catholic. What I remember, and mourn, is the blurred joyousness of a day that smelled of incense and grandmothers' perfume and that centered on the alternately squalling or sleeping baby carried about by a succession of guardians, and wearing the same trailing white gown worn by all the previous babies and sure to be worn by the next one as well— there being proof in the purpose and excitement of the day that we were all meant to be, and all welcomed.

Some comparable recollection lodges in the memory of most of the parents I talked to, warring, as they do in me, with present circumstances and convictions, yet exerting surprising force—like a scene out of a Ralph Lauren ad, and equally unattainable. "When I was growing up," said Wendy Kaufman, "religion to me was boring. It was just what my family did on Sundays. After my dad died, they took us to my grandparents, in Youngstown, Ohio. My grandparents were not very devout people but they believed that people went to church on Sunday. Grandfather took us and Grandmother stayed home and made a big two o'clock dinner. We had been Congregationalists until Daddy died, but my grandparents were Methodists, and it was very different. When I was eleven years old, I became famous in my family for refusing to go to church. I said the people were hypocrites. I remember picking up the phrase somewhere, from someone who used it. Because Dale's father is a Baptist minister, when Whitney was small we began taking her to his parents' church. She would go to Sunday school while we visited.

In one way, it accomplished one of my goals, to have a sense of family and *extended* family that had to do with rituals and some sort of standards and comforts for one's fears—the comfort of being with one's parents and grand-parents. But there was also the problem of what I took to be a somewhat barbaric theology. The early Bible stories are very sweet, but later it was going to get complicated. I wanted her to have something else, which is why I chose the Unitarians. I like the idea of the family attending church together. I just don't like most churches. I love the idea of Sunday being devoted to high purpose, great music, lovely thoughts—that sort of dipping back to pre–Daddy dying. A lovely day."

Sally Shea described her attachment to the traditions of religion in strikingly similar terms. "I don't go to church regularly, but I wish I went more than I do," she said. "It brings me back to a place where I was very secure, when you're eight years old and Mommy and Daddy are there. Last summer, Kelly would go to mass with my mother every day. She'd say, 'Grandma, I can't understand what's going on.' So my mother bought her the same white prayer book we had as kids. She's making her First Communion next month. We had to go out and get the dress—it was just like the ones we wore—and the slip and the white shoes. I love ritual. I would have made a great British subject."

Yet another woman I talked to told me she thought she was indifferent to the whole business until I happened to call her to arrange an interview—at which moment she suddenly remembered a dream she had had recently, in which she had smuggled her daughter into a spare bedroom to have her baptized by a clergyman friend without her husband's knowledge. In accounts that ranged from comic to bitter, I heard from a variety of parents who were themselves raised as Catholics but who no longer practice, of trying to arrange baptism for their children either to please grandparents or satisfy their own need for ritual, only to be scolded or sent packing by the local parish priest for want of proper credentials. A few parents spoke of "naming" ceremonies—bloodless substitutes for the bris or baptism one is not willing to have. Others dated their last formal association with the church of their childhood to some such ceremony.

"Talk about irrationality," recalled Muriel Hall of her daughter's baptism some forty years ago in the Episcopal church in which her father was a priest, a grandfather and a brother bishops. "Here's an example of the old sentimental thing. *I* was baptized on Holy Innocents Day, which was three days after Christmas. So here I was, planning to have Becka baptized on the Day of Innocents. I no longer believed in church. I had already decided I was a deist—having passed through my atheist phase and my agnostic phase—and I knew what I thought about all the religious claptrap. So here I was, going through this all for purely sentimental reasons. How do you explain it? We used the top layer of our wedding cake for a christening cake, we bought lovely champagne. People gave her christening gifts. You have to understand, I could not get away with *not* baptizing her without causing a rift, but in doing it, we really did it. And after that we made no attempt to raise Becka in any religion. Sundays we did as we pleased—went boating or whatever."

A similar seizure of form took hold of Richard Gallin when his first son was born. He had given no thought to the question ahead of time, but as soon as he heard he had a son, he realized he wanted a proper bris performed at home, not a hospital circumcision. Having no synagogue affiliation at the time, he got the name of a professional *mohel* from the hospital pediatrician, called the man up and arranged to have him come to their apartment for the traditional ceremony on the baby boy's eighth day. The morning of the bris, the *mohel* called back to make sure Gallin had on hand all the items necessary. You have to have gauze, he told him, you have to have Vaseline, you have to have ten Jewish men. They had the gauze and the Vaseline, but counting himself, his father, and his father-in-law, Gallin realized they had only three Jewish men. With the *mohel* due to arrive any minute, he ran down to the first floor of his apartment building and began working his way back up, knocking on doors in search of seven cooperative strangers, seven cooperative Jewish male strangers. By the time the *mohel* arrived, he had succeeded in assembling the requisite minyan, and his son was in short order initiated into the ancient community of Israel.

To some extent, the desire to partake of the rituals of one's childhood faith is a reflection of the desire to maintain identity and tradition and continue it through one's children. But it is equally a reflection of the human need to mark moments of individual and cultural significance, aspects of life for which we have few secular substitutes— or, at any rate, few substitutes as emotionally satisfying as those refined over centuries by religion. One can be married in a garden or a living room, or as we saw more frequently than seems possible in recent years, while free-falling from a plane or scuba diving. One can be tossed in a potter's field or scattered upon the waves after death. But most of us hope for some grace note to accompany our passage through life, for some ceremony to attend our common holidays and, more importantly, to give meaning to our children's lives.

"I feel vaguely unsatisfied whenever I think about this," said Sarah Lang. "No matter what I think about it, I feel like a fraud. I feel uneasy about whether to celebrate Christmas. But Eastertime is the worst for me, because it meant so much to me once. Now Easter morning comes and goes, Emily gets her basket, and that's it."

"It always comes up around Passover," another woman told me. A "cultural" Jew married to a nonpracticing Christian, she had responded to my first mention of the subject by saying she wouldn't be a good person to talk to because "we do nothing about religion in our family." She had grown up without religion and was raising her son the same way. And yet she was not immune to the pull of ritual. "Every year," she said, "we go to a seder at the house of the only friends of mine who are totally unconflicted about religion, and I love it, and Christopher loves it, and I start to think, maybe. Then I catch myself and I say, there is no way that I could do this."

It is one of the many contradictions of the present age that churchgoers and those indifferent or opposed to organized worship share a culture that is at once relentlessly secular and full to overflowing with religious imagery, metaphor, and art. Religious reference is so ubiquitous as to be largely unconscious, but the words and phrases incorporated into secular speech are for the most part as isolated from their original power and meaning as a West African mask on a museum wall. Thus we order "Bloody Marys" in bars (and on conservative outings, "Virgin Marys"), speak of being "born again" when embarking on a new diet, affix the word "miracle" to every unpredicted bit of good luck and every household product that does what it advertises; we sprinkle our speech liberally with "godawfuls" and "God Bless You's," dream of "greener pastures," and "the promised land," sigh over our "crosses" in life.

In certain contexts and certain voices, the metaphors ring true, bespeaking a background steeped not just in religious terminology but in comprehension. When Jim Lehrer, in describing efforts to streamline the PBS news hour of which he is cohost is quoted as saying, "For me, it was a little bit like going down to the altar again and getting renewed," one can picture those round, unblinking eyes taking in scene after scene of spiritual drama as a boy. And when saxophonist Branford Marsalis, speaking of going up against jazz elder Sonny Rollins in a jam session, says, "I'll be the lamb on that altar, because someday I'll be sixty and I'll be sacrificing some kid, too," one assumes he picked up the image not in a comparative religion course but in a lifetime of churchgoing.

Yet it is equally apparent that neither widespread familiarity with the Bible nor acquaintance with particular religious traditions can any longer be assumed. In the space of two days recently, I was told by a professor of literature at a private university that not a single student in a class in which he was teaching Gabriel García Márquez's Love in the Time of Cholera had any notion what Pentecost was about, and by a journalist teaching a course in communications at a large state university, that not one in a class of twenty students had ever read parts of the Bible.

Though such stories seem like material for a sequel to E. D. Hirsch's *Cultural Literacy,* they by no means describe a sudden collapse of educational or religious standards, only the continuance of a process that has been underway for a long time. The 1950s, for instance, tend to be remembered by most people as a period of cultural and religious conformity, when children and their parents had closer acquaintance with the verities, and with the traditions that attended them. In fact, the week before Christmas 1954, the Gallup organization issued the results of a "nationwide religion quiz" that revealed a God-fearing nation badly in need of a religious almanac.

Then, as now, roughly half the country attended church weekly and all but a handful claimed belief in God, yet only one adult in a hundred correctly answered all ten questions, beginning with "Who was the mother of Jesus?" While 95 percent of those questioned managed to come up with the right answer to that one (Mary), matters rapidly deteriorated. Only 64 percent correctly named the town where Jesus was born (the quiz was looking for Bethlehem as the correct answer, though biblical scholarship has since pointed toward Nazareth, the town where Jesus is believed to have grown up), and only 49 percent could name the first book of the Bible (Genesis). "What is the Holy Trinity?" was correctly answered by 40 percent (Father, Son, and Holy Ghost—or Spirit); "What country ruled Jerusalem during the time of Jesus?" (Rome) by 35 percent; and "Who delivered the Sermon on the Mount?" (Jesus) by 34 percent. Fewer than one person in three could name "the founder of one other religion besides Christianity," ("Buddha, Mohammed, Confucius, etc." was the answer listed), and only 21 percent could identify "one of the prophets mentioned in the Old Testament of the Bible" (a dozen major and minor prophets were listed, among them Isaiah, Jeremiah, Ezekiel, Daniel, Amos, and Hosea). The penultimate question included the hint that "One person wrote most of the books of the New Testament," but only 19 percent could name him (Paul), while the last question proved fatal to even the highest early scorers. Only 5 percent of those asked—half of them clergy, I suspect—could say what "the initials 'IHS' stand for."

This last, I would argue, as someone who more or less knows the answer, is a bit obscure for a "basic" quiz. Even the most devout of Catholics, after all, having stared pointblank at hundreds of different renditions of the holy monogram through a lifetime of masses and benedictions—the three letters picked out in gold thread against the green or scarlet or bright blue silk of the priest's chasuble, embroidered in interlocking gothic letters of black or red against the white of the altar cloth—might well confuse the Greek initials for Christ with some country club insignia, or a young bride's trousseau markings.

None of this would surprise Lynn Westfield, the Riverside Church Sunday school's director. "Who is Lazarus?" she interrupted herself to ask rhetorically as we talked about the difficulty of educating children to religious literacy and religious imagination in the secular world. "Children don't hear any of it at home anymore. It's a dying part of our culture."

"If you think about who are the keepers of our stories,"

Westfield went on, "it has always been the grandparents. But children are no longer surrounded by extended families. Our entertainment used to be storytelling, but sacred stories are not part of the telling any longer. Now we have TV, VCRs. I watch cartoons, as part of my job, so I'll know what the children are seeing. The oral tradition was always fluid, and creative. It let you conjure up what you needed. When the storytelling became visual, it was no longer so intimate or personal. We have replaced our images with somebody else's image. Once that happens, there's no longer room there for *mine*. *They* have the power of the image. In the oral tradition, the people had the power of the image. Now capitalist America has the power."

Westfield's point is, of course, applicable to every aspect of children's imaginative lives. They are flooded with characters and playthings that are not open-ended but defined to the last detail. The most popular dolls for girls now come equipped with prepared histories, "lifestyles," stories. Not dolls but Barbie Dolls, Cabbage Patch Kids, Samantha, Molly, or Kirsten. Boys play not with a sack of marbles but sitting at a computer screen. Yet the argument can be stretched in either direction. Children are wonderfully skilled at redirecting whatever comes their way to satisfy their concerns at play: a pair of Barbies is easily pressed into service as mother and daughter, teacher and student, doctor and patient; so are space stations constructed from Lincoln Logs and kazoos turned into forbidden guns. With equal proprietariness, children garble and redirect religious imagery and religious figures to suit their momentary needs.

One afternoon I overheard my daughter and her friend

Kate playing in the living room. Inspired by a ceramic holy water font I had bought in Italy and that had just arrived in the mail, they had decided to "play religion." Using the coffee table as an altar, they intoned some made-up words over the assembled plates and cups. There was much bobbing of heads and then suddenly my daughter called to me. "What religion uses holy water? Is it Catholics or Jews?" When I explained that Catholics are the ones who use holy water, the two of them nodded and started back to their game. Then Kate, both of whose parents had long since forgone the practice of their respective religions, turned back to me and added, "Well, I could play either way, because I'm half Jewish and half Catholic."

That sacred practices and terms should become the materials of play, or that children rather easily mistake the sacred for the secular, and vice versa, should not come as a surprise. Even within the convention of belief, the customs of a given religion take some getting used to. Those of an unfamiliar denomination are likely to appear arbitrary and mystifying to the uninitiated. When the choreography of the Catholic mass was subtly altered in her parish church in the late 1960s, my annoyed aunt complained, "All this standing up and sitting down at the wrong places, we might as well be Lutherans!" Such fine distinctions are totally lost on my daughter, whose frame of reference for religious conduct has been pieced together through visits to an assortment of different churches attended by friends or family members, all of them blending into some approximate image of bowed heads, reverent hand gestures, and repeated rearrangements in the pews in response to musical or other cues.

Thus tutored in the ritual arts, she was ready for the moment when the television cameras zoomed in on Cincinnati Reds manager Lou Pinella during the World Series a couple of years ago and caught him flashing batting and base signals to his players from the dugout. "Look," she said to me in surprise. "He's praying!" Which, after a fashion, of course, he was.

> "When Seth was in the Unitarian Sunday
> school in Houston, his class had the
> traditional pageant at Christmas, and he
> played the part of Joseph. But it was
> a very curious pageant, because it started
> with cavemen and the winter solstice.
> The story of Christ was just one more myth."
>
> —Lyn Geeslin

As a shaping element of culture, religion has both a long reach and a broad one. It borrows and bestows with roughly equal energy. Secular themes and celebrations are continually being absorbed into the religious calendar, religious imagery and figures recycled for secular use. Easter is far from being the only "borrowed" feast in the Christian calendar; in fact, it was not until the fourth century after Christ that the winter solstice and the associated Roman festival of lights were appropriated to celebrate the birth of Christ. What the actual date might be has been a matter of speculation since earliest Christian times (one suggestion was May 20, according to the *Dictionary of World Religions*) but it is no more the twenty-fifth of December than the Queen of England's is the first of June.

The choice of December 25, however, a date established

by Roman emperor Aurelian a century earlier as the
"Birthday of the Invincible Sun" was shrewdly inspired,
a reworking of the existing symbolism of light and hope
that managed to convey the full power of the Christian
message. What could be more thrilling, or more universally welcomed, than the appearance in the gloom of
deepest winter of a newborn savior—the "light of the
world"? Thus was the "Invincible Sun" transformed into
God's invincible son, and the very reckoning of time
adjusted to the fact of his birth.

This pattern of religious "plagiarism," as one disaffected Catholic friend of mine describes it with understandable annoyance—it is hard, after all, for those
brought up in the "one and only" true faith to discover,
as he put it, "that *everybody* had a virgin birth going"—
and its close relative, the secularization of the sacred,
recurs so frequently as to be culturally invisible most of
the time.

Approaching the six or seven weeks between Thanksgiving and New Year's that has come to be called "the
holiday season," for example, a friend invited me to attend a session of a support group of corporate women
who meet periodically to discuss the difficulties of com-
bining motherhood with full-time work outside the
home. The subject for this meeting, which took place in
mid-autumn, was "How Important Is a Spiritual Life?"
but before the scheduled discussion began, over lunch
around a twenty-foot conference table, each woman gave
a brief account of herself—her job, how long she had
been working, the age and gender of her children, and
so forth. And as one woman after another spoke, it became obvious that what they really wanted to talk about

was Halloween, which had just passed a few days before.

Far from being a minor event, the children's holiday appeared to have taken on enormous significance in the lives of these mothers, and their descriptions of the preparations and the actual event were delivered with the sort of animation and detail women traditionally reserve for tales of love or childbirth. One after another, they told how their children had decided what they were going to "be" for Halloween, how they, the mothers, had then assembled or sewn the appropriate costumes, how they had left work early or made special arrangements with the baby-sitter to take the child trick-or-treating. It was clear that this holiday satisfied these women in a way no other celebration did and eventually the conversation shifted toward why that should be. One woman suggested that it was because Halloween was what she called a "true children's day"; a second, that the element of make-believe made it especially fun; and a third, that, unlike Thanksgiving, for example, it did not entail messy involvement with one's troublesome extended family, and a wretched meal to boot. Though no two of the women present had joined forces for the special day, by telling about it afterward, they managed to turn the event into something resembling a communal rite, an experience the subsequent discussion would establish as a rare event in their lives. And finally, one woman said that what she liked about it was that it was a purely secular holiday—that, unlike Easter or Christmas or Passover, it did not make you feel uncomfortable about choices not made.

Everyone around the table nodded in agreement. Then I noticed a few faces registering confusion as their owners

struggled to recall just where this wonderful holiday did
come from. Feeling something of a pedant, but encouraged by the official subject of the day, I volunteered that
while it was technically not a religious feast itself, Halloween did derive from one, being the eve of All Saints'
(or All Hallows') Day in the Christian calendar—*hallow*
meaning holy, as in "hallowed be Thy name." The gob-
lins and ghosts, devils and broom-riding witches, now
rapidly being displaced by fairy princesses, astronauts,
and Ninja Turtles, refer to a long tradition of caricature
of the unholy dead, as well as to Celtic pagan traditions
that antedate Christianity and have to do with the onset
of winter's darkness and the unleashing of emotions cus-
tomarily repressed. This bit of information was politely
received, but generated no further discussion. Not only
were these women not much interested in Halloween's
religious antecedents; there could be little doubt but that
their sense of the holiday as a thoroughly secular one was
both an active preference and a proper gauge of general
sentiment.

Halloween does indeed have a special resonance for
parents and children, but it no longer has much of anything to do with its ancient and layered origins.* Children
dressing up as pirates or Darth Vader or ballet dancers—
even as devils or ghosts—are not playing with religious
ideas but engaging in secular fantasy and satisfying a more
recent and secular tradition. In doing what their parents

---

*Ironically, while the majority of Christians celebrate Halloween with-
out a thought to its once considerable religious significance, the Jewish
day school one of my friend's children attends sends a note home
every October to remind parents that it is a Christian holiday and that
their children should not be participating in it.

did before them as children—something they are very rarely encouraged or allowed to do—children fulfill the most basic requirements of tradition, which are repetition and continuance. Parents who are both starved for ritual and who mourn the passing of what they remember as a simpler time can for this one day imagine that their children are as innocent as they would like them to be; they can imagine that their own lives, which are, in reality, vastly different from those led by *their* parents, have some ritual continuity. Halloween, meanwhile, like some patch of jungle that has been cleared for a time and lovingly cultivated only to be left fallow again, has reverted to something close to its pagan origins, leaving behind only the faintest traces of the sacred to be scoured for meaning.

In much the same way we have transformed a Near Eastern bishop of the fourth century into Santa Claus— the jolly fellow with the sack of toys without whose commerical enthusiasm the modern retail economy would collapse in a heap. An immensely popular saint in the early Christian Church, Saint Nicholas was counted the special patron of several different Christian countries, as well as of sailors everywhere, but was especially venerated as the patron of children, parents, and fertility. He was forever popping up to rescue poor children or intervene happily in the fates of virgins. In one of the many legends of his largesse, he deposits golden dowries beside three poor maidens as they sleep. Though Bruno Bettelheim, in *A Good Enough Parent,* cites this detail as foretelling his eventual reputation as an unseen, or anonymous, midnight gift-giver, it can also be read as a somewhat pointed metaphor for conception itself, nicely merging with the many traditions linking Saint Nicholas with fertility.

As it also echoes the appearance of the three Magi bearing gifts to the Christ Child, the symbolic dovetailing would seem to be indefinitely continuable. In fact, Saint Nicholas's symbolic richness has accommodated many different traditions over the centuries as people have made of him what they like, layering him with local customs and locally appealing idiosyncrasies. In many countries his feast day, December 6, remains distinct from Christmas Day, a day of gift-giving attended by its own set of rituals. For American children, however, who acquired him by way of their Dutch neighbors in colonial times (Santa Klaus)—and thereby were spared the no-frills Christmas they would otherwise have inherited from their Puritan forebears—he is as firmly attached to December 25 as the baby Jesus, though utterly dissociated from his religious origins. He is the secular counterpart for the season, a generic figure on whom most any benign sentiment can be hung without penalty: he can be toy-making elf, pipe-smoking grandfather, absentminded buffoon, indulgent parent, even, if you will, a blackmailer of good cheer—"You better not pout." He is not Saint Anybody anymore but a fellow in red who lives about as far from Asia Minor as time and imagination can arrange.

The emphasis so many parents place on this secular Santa Claus's "reality," on the other hand, reflects an undiminished need to anchor our Christmas celebrations in myth. Even as they waffle on the subject of who exactly the babe in the manger is, parents are free to insist, for as long as the child will buy it, that Santa Claus really does the extraordinary things they say he does. For many of the parents I spoke to, this belief in Santa Claus's reality stands as the last defense against the loss of innocence they fear means the end of a childhood already too short by far, and it permits a collusion of fantasy between parent and child that more serious issues of religious belief do not. "I'd like my kids to believe in Santa Claus for as long as possible," said Robin Glazer, "and I think they want to believe as well. Every year my husband and I make baby powder footprints leading into the living room on Christmas Eve. Last year, I heard my eleven-year-old and my seven-year-old arguing about whether they were real or not. The younger one was saying they were just powder, but the older one was insisting on snow. He really wanted to believe."

Dan Menaker, another nonbeliever, made much the same point. "I'd like my son to believe in Santa Claus, and the tooth fairy, as long as they delight him," adding, "If you don't give them such figures, children will invent them anyway." As for the inevitable disillusionment to come, Menaker said, "As I recall, casting aside the idea of Santa Claus given to me by my atheistic parents was not a big deal. We go from one belief system to another in terms of readiness. I also think," he said, "that it may be instructive to kids in that it shows them that they shouldn't believe everything their parents tell them."

For Candace Burnett, such skepticism came too late to distinguish those holiday figures she was meant to believe in only temporarily and the one she was supposed to believe in permanently. "They told me there was Jesus Christ, Santa Claus, and the Easter Bunny, and that Jesus was born at the time of Santa Claus and died at the time of the Easter Bunny. And then they told me there was no Santa Claus and there was no Easter Bunny—well, there went Jesus Christ out the window."

Dissociated as they may be from their original religious

content, traditions remain at the service of the human instinct to celebrate and to commune, to mark the passage of time and to connect past and present through repetition, to frame ordinary life by extraordinary observance. But observance of what? *Something* special must happen in the long night of winter, just as some festivity must welcome the coming of spring. It was in large part the nagging inadequacy of a Christmas without Christ at its center that finally pushed Sue Gilger to return to church when her children were young, but even for parents who cannot bring themselves to tell their children that the infant Jesus is literally the offspring of God and a virgin named Mary, Christmas represents more than just an emotion-laden replay of their own childhoods. To elevate the day and the season above the runaway materialism so many claim to dread, some redeeming fable needs to be told, if not *the* fable; some icon placed at the center of the celebration, if not *the* icon.

"Of course you have a Christmas stocking and a creche at Christmas," said Katharine Bouton, who was raised as an Episcopalian, and for whom, despite adult nonbelief, both Christmas and Easter remain important holidays. "In some sense, they wouldn't exist if I didn't go to church," she says, acknowledging the apparent, and widely shared, inconsistency of her position. As to why the birth of this particular babe continues to be celebrated so spectacularly, "I say," she began, "that Jesus was a very holy man . . . and that some people believe he was God. I also say that at the time he was born, people who believed he was God thought that the appearance of a very bright star over Bethlehem was a miracle that had to do with him being God."

In some such form did the majority of nonreligious

parents I talked to explain their accounting of Christmas to their children, some combination of folklore and reverence that sidesteps theological precision yet attempts to preserve the sense of something extraordinary being celebrated. Among Unitarians, whose synthesis of tradition and humanism attempts to preserve the celebratory aspects of religion absent their obvious, and controversial, implications, the preferred circumlocution for the Nativity is "the birth of a special baby." As if promulgated in the cultural ether, it turns out to be the private, ad hoc solution arrived at by many nonbelieving parents eager to invest the holiday with some significance for their children beyond a surfeit of presents.

"The Christmas tree has sort of become my religion," is how Jonina Herter put it. "I have a collection of beautiful ornaments, and decorating the tree is an important ritual for us. But," she added, "I recently went out and bought a creche, too. We celebrate the birth of a special baby." So, in a limited way, does Penny Coleman's family. "We have no creche in the house," she says, "but they see one at my mother's. They think the baby Jesus is a good guy."

To Suzzy Roche, a singer who organizes a benefit for homeless women each Christmas, the point of Christmas is what it causes us to reflect on. "I tell my daughter that some people believe that Jesus was the son of God, but that no one really knows for sure, and that it doesn't really matter whether it is true or not. What matters is the idea of honoring someone who was born poor and who had nothing in the world, who had no place to go. And to realize that there are still people who have no place to go, and are excluded." "Sammy loves the baby Jesus," said another mother, moved by the tenderness with which her son viewed the vulnerable newborn in a manger. "That's really what matters."

It is possible to take a deeply pessimistic view of the secularization of a once-significant religious holiday such as Christmas and to read into it a more general misuse of religious ritual that threatens to reduce it to mere diversion, a form of seasonal entertainment. A more realistic reading would begin by acknowledging that for a great many people in the modern world, the gap between the holidays as we celebrate them and the metaphysical riddles they originally expressed has widened unbridgeably. And yet the pull of ritual, and the desire to celebrate special experiences and special days, remains immensely powerful. As someone who felt herself utterly cut off from any kind of ceremonial life as a child, for instance, Robin Glazer confesses to having spent much of her adult life consciously compensating. "Neither of my parents spoke Yiddish or in any way acted on their Jewishness," she recalls, "but we still were not allowed to have a Christmas tree when I was growing up. The minute I moved out of my mother's house I got my own tree. I got books on how to make Swedish ornaments and Mexican ornaments. I had a tree-decorating party. But I also remember coming to the table as a child with a Haggadah and hoping to 'pull off' a Passover. It was not religious feeling but me wanting to have a family that performed rituals. It had to do with the joyousness of being a child. That's what ritual is for me, and why I am constantly providing it for my kids. I want them to have it all— Easter eggs, the tooth fairy, Santa Claus."

While one could argue that such an appropriation of

ritual without reference to its underlying or original significance bespeaks nothing more compelling than simple consumerism, it also argues for the irresistibility of holidays for families, and of the importance of celebration. If need be, new definitions of specialness will be invented, old ones reimagined or reinvested with slightly altered meanings. In the divinity schools, they argue the divinity of Christ; in popular mythology, the question is increasingly beside the point.

"We used to feel sorry for people who sent nonreligious Christmas cards," Muriel Hall recalls of her childhood, as I certainly recall of mine. But it may be asking too much to expect consistency on such matters. At the same time as fastidious ex-believers like myself can no longer bring themselves to mail out a traditional Madonna and Child at year's end, a friend who was raised as an atheist in a succession of small towns in an era when a creche on the courthouse lawn or a Christmas tree on the public school stage went unremarked and unobjected to, quietly begrudges their absence in her own child's life. In any abstract intellectual discussion, she would defend the separation of church and state with ferocity; emotionally, she wishes her son's public school would stage a proper pageant, with shepherds, wise men, and a shining gold star overhead. Christmas carols would follow.

Possibly as significant as whether one's celebrations are founded in true belief is the degree to which they increasingly take a private shape. Throughout history, in most parts of the world, religion and culture have been one—and to a great degree remain so, even, as in most of Western Europe, where religious practice itself is close to vestigial. In France, Spain, and Italy, for example, where church attendance is a fraction of what it is among American Catholics, everything nevertheless shuts down on August 15 each year as socialist heads of government troop to mass and their countrymen and women take to the beach in honor of the Feast of the Assumption.

For the majority of contemporary believers in this country, however, except for Christmas, when schools and businesses alike close down, there is no such link between religious observance and the rest of one's life. A procession through the streets is not a community event but an isolated performance of the private rites of a particular group come together for this one event. The devout speak disparagingly of Easter Catholics or High Holiday Jews, but the more remarkable thing may be that so many manage to make the connection at all. Of whatever importance to the individual it remains, religious ceremony is no longer routinely integrated into community life. Indeed, one of the most surprising things I learned when I began interviewing parents was how rarely religious community and the rest of one's life— one's circle of friends and neighbors, professional associates or even blood relatives—came together. While many recalled childhoods in which religion and community were essentially synonymous ("My parents have no friends outside their congregation," Randall Balmer told me), it was not an experience circumstances permit most to repeat. "None of my friends are raising their kids as Catholics," said Sally Shea.

Again and again, as parents described their search for a church or a synagogue to join—for the sake of a Sunday school, the opportunity to worship, or out of tradition— they described an ideological quest or, almost as frequently, a geographic convenience, but almost never a natural alignment by community. Further evidence of this pattern of isolation turns up in a survey conducted by the National Opinion Research Center in Chicago in 1988, in which respondents were asked to name three close friends other than their spouses, and indicate whether any of them belonged to the same congregation as the respondent. Only one in four answered yes with respect to the first "good" friend, while the percentage dropped even lower for friends number two and three.

To some extent this is a simple reflection of America's religious pluralism; the dominant "Christian tradition" in American life has always been a patchwork tradition, with new denominations continually springing up to claim the allegiance of the disaffected, and the difference between one's neighbor's church and one's own likely to be greater than one's political differences. Fewer and fewer of us, meanwhile, belong any longer to communities destined to outlive us and into which we must fit ourselves; rather we take membership, sequentially, and for a limited time, in a series of small interest groups. We are schoolchildren or senior citizens, single or married, parents or not, but we are seldom citizens together, townspeople, members of a congregation or of any embracing community. We do not gather round the maypole on the green, we do not bring in the harvest or raise barns. Our addresses and our allegiances are equally subject to change (even, as in the case of sports heroes, against our will).

Reflecting on the remarkable resurgence of patriotism that attended the early phase of the recent war with Iraq, psychiatrist Willard Gaylin, president of the Hastings

Center, spoke of how the war "played into the need for community." It was not, he argued, simple jingoism at work, or a thirst for war, but rather a "hunger for some integrating force for our lives." It is painful to live without a sense of community, but it is how most Americans now live. And ritual, one of the guarantors of community, has become increasingly fragmented or marginalized. All disasters, natural or man-made, Gaylin said, put us "in touch with other people." When the war finally began, after being heralded for weeks like some hurricane gathering force offshore, it did, in fact, briefly make us a community, simply because, as Gaylin said, "We were all watching the same thing."

That what we were all watching was war was a point oddly overlooked by some, but there was no denying that the experience of sharing the moment was exhilarating. It was an authentic communal event, like the week following President Kennedy's assassination or the San Francisco earthquake of 1989, and for a short time one did not have to guess what one's neighbors were thinking about. One knew. Conversations between strangers became commonplace, and just as "What's the score?" does not require a preamble during the World Series, so "Has it started?" did not require one the week of January 15.

In the course of my research for this book, I attended a wide variety of church services, plain and fancy, routine and special. What appeared equally obvious in the best and the worst orchestrated of services, and in the best and worst attended, was how eager many of the participants were to be there—to sing and to pray in unison, to parade, to stand and sit as one, or to step out from the group to perform a special function.

At an incense-clouded service in an Episcopal cathedral that might have served as a backdrop to a coronation, I watched a woman in late middle age as she teetered toward the altar on high-heeled white go-go boots; beaming a look of fixed joy, she carried a chalice full of papery, wheaten hosts for the priest to consecrate. In a Catholic church in San Jose, home to a mix of urban professionals and recent Asian immigrants, I witnessed an adult baptism featuring total body immersion during Holy Thursday services—an event unimaginable to generations of Catholics accustomed to liturgical decorum, but so perfectly in tune with the reinvented ceremony as to seem as timeless and unalterable as the Mass itself once did. At an orthodox bar mitzvah, I watched a neighbor and his son as they took their places in the *bimah,* the enclosure reserved for men in the center of the synagogue, slipping on their tefillin and tallis before prayer like athletes outfitting themselves before a game, their assuredness in their roles and this place beyond doubt. One balmy Palm Sunday, I joined the congregation of a large and prosperous suburban Baptist church as its members filled the pews to overflowing, the choir in handsome, brightly colored robes, the worshippers dressed in a splendor that surpassed their surroundings. In another, smaller, Episcopal church, I have several times watched my own unbaptized daughter, robed in red, carrying the cross in a procession of small children, her unofficial inclusion a courtesy of the generous and ever-hopeful Sunday school teacher. I am simultaneously charmed and stone-hearted; I find I want to pull her aside and tell her of the processions *we* used to throw. I am, of course, too guilty to do that and wish that there were some nonliturgical way I could ar-

range for her to wear flowers in her hair in May and
parade around a courtyard the way her mother and aunts
did when they were small.

Not everyone pines equally for the rising flumes of
incense and accompanying organ, of course. Even among
Catholics, who are presumed to have enjoyed some
golden devotional past, there are many whose memories
do not include vaulting naves, Renaissance-inspired art
over the altar, or music worth sitting through sermons
for. "I was not raised with the 'better music' and the
'better art,' " said Sarah Lang. "By the time I was exposed
to it, I was irritated by it, because it reminded me of what
I had not liked about Catholicism in other respects. For
a long time, I felt very bitter about having been raised in
a Catholicism that was very primitive and narrow. A
couple of times when I was in crisis as an adult, I went
into a church in hopes of feeling some connection, but I
felt it had nothing to do with my life."

Like opera, religious ritual operates within conventions
that can seem meaningless or ridiculous out of context.
"People sitting around singing make me very uncomfortable," said Jo Ann Sickinger, who views the whole
business of religion from the perspective of a lifelong
outsider. "I feel very vulnerable to the emotions it un-
leashes. I feel it in movies too, everybody sitting there
together crying, like in *Field of Dreams*. I feel a bit ma-
nipulated."

A childhood spent in the bosom of the Methodist
church—much of it as a precocious church organist—
gave Campbell Geeslin an intense distaste for religion's
aesthetic coercion. "I am very suspicious of ritual," he
said. "*Especially* if it moves me emotionally—then I really

distrust it. I feel I don't want that from religion, whatever religion is. I like it fine in the theater and in movies, but not in church. Through many centuries of experience, they have figured out what gets people. And they use it with some kind of calculation that I find very off-putting. It's not spontaneous. Of course, a theatrical production isn't either. But the purpose is not the same." To which his wife, Lyn, having grown up under much less religious pressure, and recalling some fond memories of Chartres Cathedral and what she called an experience of "vicarious religion," asked him, "But if the idea *is* to move you?"

"But that's just it," he insisted. "I don't want to be moved by religion. At all."

Being moved, of course, is exactly what most others do want, and they are as grateful for the calculation, or the inspired art, that makes the spirit soar as for any moral prescriptives or putative guarantees concerning the hereafter. "If I were going to become Christian again," said Jonina Herter, who grew up suspended between Catholicism and Protestantism, "I would become Episcopalian. I would require the trappings, the formality I remember from Catholicism, but in English. I'd like a quiet place to think, to puzzle out the mysteries. I like churches— the space and the physical grandeur. I like high ceilings and echoey places. I wouldn't mind sitting in one."

It is not an accidental effect. "The Archangel loved heights," begins *Mont-Saint-Michel and Chartres,* Henry Adams's classic study of the intersection of art and religion. "Like all great churches," Adams writes, "Chartres expressed, besides whatever else it meant, an emotion, the deepest man ever felt,—the struggle of his own littleness to grasp the infinite." It is an emotion one does not mistake, whether at the foot of a Mexican pyramid or at the center of the Stonehenge ring. Yet while they are often capable of transcending culture or time, the symbols of religion are meant nevertheless to express particular ideas, and to convey particular images. Not just exaltation or consciousness of the infinite but sacrifice, endurance, nourishment: the cross, the lamb, the dove, a flame, bread, wine, water. Except to the most scrupulously initiated, however, the evocative meaning of many of the religious symbols still in use has grown so faint as to be unreadable. The image of a lamb, for example, is central to Christian iconography. Deriving from the Judaic tradition of animal sacrifice, it represents the sacrificial victim of Jesus Christ, lamb of God. In the secular imagination, however, the lamb carries only the connotation of innocence; it is a creature of the nursery rhyme—victimizable, to be sure, but not sacred, and not a terribly potent symbol for city dwellers. Similarly, the image of the fish, which still adorns altar linens and liturgical vestments, was a symbol for Christ in the early underground church, but as I watched one beleagured Sunday school teacher attempt to interest his distracted pupils in the significance of their persecuted ancestors drawing fish in the Roman dust with their sandaled feet, I had to wonder how much longer it will survive in anyone's religious vocabulary—except for those practicing astrology.

"He's so fabulously ignorant," said one old friend of the son she chose to raise without religious education of any kind in a small town in Washington state. "I was picking him up at school one day and the car of someone we know slightly was parked in front of me and it had one of those Christian fish decals on the back of it, like people put next to their names in the phonebook out here. As we're driving out of the parking lot, I'm ranting and raving about this display and how I didn't know they were *those* kind of people, and my son turns to me and he says, 'So what is that, Pisces?' "

Either the ancient images must be explicated—a major business of preachers in the modern day—or new symbols with more vital meanings must be devised. In effect, this is happening all the time, though with predictably uneven results.

On a visit to a Unitarian church one day, I was surprised to learn from the minister that an oversized mosaic depicting Jesus washing the feet of his disciples was a source of discomfort for many in the congregation. Despite the fact that this particular detail from the Last Supper emphasizes Christ's example of humility, the all-male, all-white cast of characters struck many of the church's members as inappropriate, and discussions were under way to figure out how to replace or obscure it with some more acceptable image.

A year or so later, I happened to notice a short article in a local newspaper titled "Historic Church Gets New Figleaf," and discovered that Jesus and the Apostles had indeed been draped. "What bothered them," the article reported, "was that the image, which harkens back to the white male dominant nineteenth century theological view . . . might somehow offend members and friends of the church who do not share these attributes of color and gender.

"Berger [the minister] explains that church members and friends also could not agree on putting up [any of] the myriad symbols of the world's faiths for fear of giving offense, say, to an Iranian Shia who might look askance at a Zoroastrian symbol as opposed to a crescent."

In search of a solution, the congregation commissioned "a large wall painting that would cover the mosaic. The result is a gold and blue spiral, an abstraction which conveys the Universalist ethos of oneness and 'shared traditions, shared thoughts.' "

Tinkering with the text in hopes of making it comprehensible to young listeners is somewhat easier to understand. Attending a Sunday school session for seven- and eight-year-olds one morning at Riverside Church, I was initially mystified by the use of a story about a "bunny" to teach the day's lesson. The story was taken from a collection called *The Way of the Wolf* by Martin Bell, which reworks the lessons of the New Testament through characters and situations presumed to "relate" more directly to children's imaginations and concerns than the Gospels in their original form. "Some of the children are very knowledgeable," explained the teacher of that day's class, a student from neighboring Union Theological Seminary, "and it's obvious that parents are reading to them from the Bible at home. But others haven't a clue."

The story read that morning was a simple story about sacrifice, though the word was never used, nor was any explicit correspondence to religious material made. It told of a rabbit named Barrington, a somewhat unusual rabbit in that he has no relatives of his own and has never even met another bunny. Barrington wishes greatly that he could meet another bunny, and at Christmastime he feels especially sorry for himself. All the other animals are hidden away with their familes for the winter and he feels lonely and useless. Along comes a silver wolf, who asks him why he is sitting in the snow.

"Because it's Christmas Eve and I have no family," Barrington replies. "Bunnies aren't any good to anyone."

"Bunnies are, too, good," says the wolf. "Bunnies can hop and they are very warm. . . . You will see why it is good to hop and to be warm and furry."

Barrington goes about the forest giving gifts to all the animals for Christmas. He signs them "from a member of your family." Later that day, it begins to snow and pretty soon it turns into a blizzard.

"It's a good thing I'm so furry," he says. Suddenly, he comes upon a baby field mouse lost and shivering in the snow. He realizes he will have to take care of it until morning. He hugs it close to his body to keep it warm, grateful that he can help another animal. "It is good to be a bunny," he says to himself. "And all of the animals in the forest are my family." In the morning, the baby mouse's family come looking for him. They find him alive and well, sheltered beneath the furry body of a rabbit frozen in the snow.

The children listening to the story sat very still throughout and were silent for a moment at the end. One or two of them seemed confused by the story's ending and asked what happened to the rabbit. "He died," several other children answered. "He froze to death."

There was no further discussion of the story, no explanation of the role of the rabbit or who the mouse might represent. It was time for clay work, and each of the children was given a lump of clay with which to make something. When I asked Lynn Westfield why the teacher had not begun a discussion about death following the story, she said it was because the children didn't ask. "We watch what they do with clay," she said. The rabbit, Westfield explained to me, represents Christ; the silver wolf represents the Holy Spirit. And sure enough, when the clay-working session was over, almost every child turned out to have modeled a dead rabbit cradling a tiny mouse.

It was a far cry from the Gospel of Saint Matthew, and I came away wondering why the animal parable was necessary. The story of the Good Samaritan, after all, would have done very well to make a similar point, or the story of Christ's sacrifice itself. Were these Disneyized stand-ins really necessary? In fact, Westfield later explained, her program uses both, alternating traditional parables with stories that carry the same messages in images closer to those of children's popular entertainment. It is not just a matter of keeping current with the competition but of making the stories accessible.

"The parables, metaphors, and images used in the Gospels are all very powerful," she said, "but they are also culturally specific, grounded in a time and culture that is unfamiliar to the children we teach. We have totally urban children here, for whom the agricultural images of the Bible are mystifying. To talk about Jesus in the desert—they've never seen a desert. They do not experience water as a life-giving substance but as something that comes out of the tap. To speak of a crop 'increasing a hundred-fold'—that doesn't mean anything to them. It just becomes a nice story. The challenge is to make them come alive in the nineties for children of a very different culture."

The particular advantage of telling a moral tale with animals, Westfield points out, is that it circumvents the sticky issues of "classism, racism, sexism, that come along as baggage." How children are taught Scripture is, of course, part of the larger debate over religious language and imagery, in which God's gender, color, and other aspects of traditional interpretation are no longer givens. It is certainly difficult to insist on the preservation of a tradition of language and symbolism in the instruction of children at a time when that tradition is being held up as anachronistic.

"To insist that the story not change over time makes no sense," Westfield argues. "The question is, how many changes can the central story absorb and remain true to its message? The core story of the Gospel is the triumph of life over death. That is what is central. But many people would like to see the metaphors used to convey that message change. Women would; black people would. For me, I want the metaphors to shift."

> "One thing that really disappointed me
> was trying to introduce my kids to religion
> as literature. I can't remember any longer which
> book of Bible stories I picked out, but I remember
> taking great care to find just the right one, and
> also a book of mythology, and I really looked forward
> to introducing my kids to this great literature. But
> they just weren't interested."
>
> —Suzanne Trazoff

Implicit in the human talent for constructive fantasy is an acknowledgment of our common need for myths to explain and transcend life as we know it—or fail to know it. Inspired by myth, the bewildered mortal can make an end run around the incomprehensibility of things to an understanding that is otherwise unattainable. If fairy tales, as Bettelheim argues in *The Uses of Enchantment,* help the child make sense of his psychological universe, religious myths (parables, legends, the lives of the saints) help him make sense of his moral universe.

One might argue that the "sense" thus arrived at needs revising, or that it is in some fundamental manner flawed, but it is not an arbitrary or accidentally arrived-at sense; it is intended, it has a purpose and a message. Few would argue, for example, that "Cinderella" is "just a story." It is quite specifically a story about longing, about alienation and betrayal, and about being rescued, as opposed to saving oneself. Some would call it a story about hope; feminists speak of it as a delusion dangerous to little girls' mental health and eventual economic well-being.

The stories of the Old Testament and the New Testament also have a clear purpose and significance beyond simple storytelling. At one level, they are *the* stories of Western culture, in which the greater part of our self-image and idealism is reflected, and from which the majority of our shaping metaphors have been formed. They happen also to detail a version of human origins and human relations that is no longer credible or acceptable to many people—in some cases, as Lynn Westfield points out, even as metaphor, and even among believers. Depending on how and what each has been taught, many parents are stuck somewhere between approval and rejection of the sometimes inconsistent lessons of scripture and the lyrical imagery in which the message is delivered. For believers, the Bible is a deep resource which parents and teachers can make use of in a variety of ways to convey universal messages of hope, endurance, sacrifice, or forgiveness. "I've always been careful to make sure the girls understand that fiction is fiction, wherever it comes from," John Winters told me. "When it comes to something like the story of Creation, I would tell them the Bible story but not stop there. I would explain the Bible stories as fiction meant to explain things by people who felt very close to God. And I think the Bible stories, the simple answers, *are* for children That's who they are meant for. You can deal with the larger questions later. They come up with all the questions: 'Why is the sky blue?' You can say, the sky is blue because God wants it that way, or you can say, because the earth revolves around the sun in this way, and so on. But I think it's important to bring God in so they'll have a concept to build on later."

For parents who do not believe, or who find one or another of the Bible's many messages troublesome, yet want their children to connect with the culture it has powerfully helped to shape, it poses a different sort of challenge.

Like most Catholics, I received a somewhat skewed biblical education, a "greatest hits" version of the Old and New Testaments, and it frankly never occurred to me to provide my daughter with a book of Bible stories to nestle on the shelf with Babar and Dr. De Soto. But when a book-reviewing friend sent us a set of *Stories of the Old and New Testament* when Anna was about three, she wanted them read to her just like any other books that came into the house. I remember sitting down with her in the living room and eyeing the twin specimens with suspicion. "Which one do you want to read first?" I asked her. She studied the two pastel illustrations for a moment before choosing the New Testament, enchanted, no doubt, by its portrait of Jesus surrounded by round-cheeked little children. I opened the book and read the first story. Whoops. Miracle number one, Jesus cures the lame. Listen, I tried to tell her, this isn't how things work. This isn't true. She looked at me queerly. I read on. Whoops, another miracle! Listen, I said, there's a problem here. I don't mind reading these, but I don't want you to believe that this is how things are. She looked at me with as much impatience as surprise. What was all this annotation business? She patted the open page. Just read, she said.

As far as she was concerned at the age of three, they were just stories. Did I turn to her in the middle of "Jack and the Beanstalk" to say, "now, *listen*—you cannot climb a beanstalk in real life. And there are no such things as giants." Did I point out in the middle of "Cinderella" that pumpkins do not become crystal coaches? What was going on here? I read on and kept my comments to myself.

Candace Burnett and Larry Small reacted somewhat more moderately when their son, Cooper, the sort of learning-besotted boy who could profitably lecture adults on fossils and dinosaurs at the age of seven, took to reading the Bible in the privacy of his room. They were struck by his abrupt but seemingly intense interest in religion, and unsure of what to make of it. "He's got this little wooden cross I built in Bible school," Candace said, "and all my old religious medals. He's created a little shrine for himself."

"I think he looks on them as good luck charms," Larry said, adding, "he's a hero worshipper. It's only natural that he'd be drawn to stories about Jesus. Remember the Harriet Tubman and the Martin Luther King books?"

"I don't think so," said Candace. "I think he has a feeling inside him that there are things that should be important. You know, when he brought home the King book and the Tubman book, we said, 'Great.' When he brought home the Bible stories, we gulped. But we backed off. He has an innate reverence." She looked at her husband. "Maybe he knows something we don't."

However one chooses to deal with questions of the Bible's literal or allegorical truth, there remains the broader question of its place and importance in the culture. The set of references, names, and allusions that were once the common coin of ordinary people is fast becoming incomprehensible. Images that would have been instantly recognizable a generation or two past are lost on the majority of adults and children today. The sort of painstaking explication needed to help non-classics students of my generation make sense of the *Iliad,* for example, is now required for the most ordinary biblical references.

"Whenever I hear someone mention Job," said one woman, "I think I wish I knew the actual story. Obviously, I don't want it badly enough to go out and study it, but I wish I knew it when I hear people talking about it."

Invite a definition of the "Tribes of Israel" or "the Marriage Feast at Cana" in any high school or college classroom and you're likely to get blank looks from all but a handful of the students. At a Christmas concert not long ago, I heard the folksinger David Massingill sing a song based on the notion of Jesus as an inmate in a modern-day insane asylum. It was a song meant, with equal parts irony, reverence, and humor, to portray Christ as too "crazy" to be listened to. The audience seemed happy to go along with the conceit—it does seem as if almost everyone still knows who Jesus is. But when he got to the line, "I think I'll go jump *on* the lake," at least half his listeners seemed not to get the joke.

Though the Bible continues to be carefully studied as a religious text within the more conservative Protestant denominations and as an elective at the college level, detailed knowledge of the Bible is increasingly isolated and arcane knowledge, something that exists outside the shared discourse of the majority—like Latin and Greek. In the preface to her elegant translation of the Old Testament for children called *The Book of Adam to Moses,* Lore Segal observes that "If this archaic work survives into the twentieth century it is because it constitutes a basic strain in our thinking. That other grand strain, the Greek, has already slipped out of our general education; the Bible is slipping because, for good and sufficient reason, it is not part of the American curriculum."

Though many of the nonreligious parents I interviewed spoke wistfully about how they wished they had given their children at least a literary appreciation of the Bible, and a few, like Suzanne Trazoff, took a stab at it, no one I talked to of my generation or younger appeared to have gotten anywhere with it. A generation earlier, however, struggling with the sense of obligation they felt to give their children some exposure to religious tradition, Muriel Hall and her husband actually succeeded.

Having been invited by some neighborhood friends, the Halls' two older children had briefly attended Sunday school at a church in their suburban New Jersey town, where their parents assumed they were being taught the rudiments of the Bible at least. Though neither she nor her husband were practicing Christians any longer, "we weren't doctrinaire," Muriel says, "and we thought it couldn't do any harm." All winter long, she remembers, "we never went near the place, and come spring, what did they bring home but wallets! That's what they had been doing all that time, making wallets. They hadn't learned anything worthwhile. Then we were asked to come to the Sunday school service one week, and we went, and there was this awful man asking people to come forward, to be saved. We were the only nonmembers as it turned out, and we decided that was the end of Sunday school.

"Eventually I talked about my predicament with a friend of my mother's who was also a practicing deist, and she said, 'Why don't you read them the Bible yourself? It's a great literary document. There's probably not a better ethic around. So raise them in it, and do it through the Bible so you can give them that, too.' So we started reading two chapters every Sunday, without fail. I remember one year we bought used bikes for the kids and we spent all one Sunday scrubbing off the rust and old paint in the basement, and that's where we read that day's chapters. I remember reading the Psalms in lovely weather, so gorgeous, the language and the beautiful days together. I remember once driving down to Princeton reading in the station wagon with the kids listening in back. And when we got to the 'begats,' it took three weeks and we almost had a rebellion, but I said we have to read them all. Just like if you haven't read the catalogue of ships in the *Iliad,* then when you get to Hector on the wall you don't really understand.

"One of the good things about doing it the way we did was that you get to do it *your* way. You don't have to accept the doctrinaire position on the stories, to have it interpreted in strict religious terms. Cain and Abel, for example, I presented as a story about conflict between the nomadic life and agricultural life. I had a couple of volumes of the *Interpreter's Bible.* And I usually used the King James exegesis for the scholarly intepretation. I could get others at work. I remember when we came across a place where they are making bronze, and I said to the kids, 'This has got to be the Bronze Age.'

"They got the history of man from the most brutal, most primitive days up to the Christian era. And you know, as Christians, you're sort of taught that the whole idea of charity and forgiveness is *yours,* but there's just about nothing Christ said that's not in the Old Testament. It made me a lot less smug."

After listening to Muriel's account, my own early skittishness on the subject struck me as foolishly reactionary, and I decided to try something similar. Free of the sense that one must be literally "bound by the miracle," as Dostoyevski has it in *The Brothers Karamazov,* it might be possible to explore the Bible as literature and as human record at least. "What I find there doesn't make me feel good about God," Lore Segal had said of her own fascination with the Bible, "but it tells us more about human nature than Freud." Having announced to my daughter that we were going to try something different one evening, I selected the lightest of the three King James versions of the Bible then sharing space on the shelf with Ronald Knox's 1944 translation, and opened to Genesis, chapter one.

"In the beginning, God created the heaven and the earth." There we were, right in it. I read on. I no longer remember just when my daughter interrupted with her first question, but I do remember that my own disposition had utterly changed. Here we were at Creation, the first big-ticket item, and I was ready for whatever came up— miracles, mysteries, contradictions, significance. What came up most was confusion, and a sort of delirium brought on by repetition, and after the first night, a lot of complaint. The same child who had proved so insatiably curious about the universe's origins and the variety of explanations people had come up with was bored by Genesis. We slogged on through a few more readings. I know we got as far as Jacob and Esau's cousin Laban, of whom I'd never heard, but we never made it to Joseph and his brothers. We had started too early, I decided, and that was probably true. She was too young. A few months later, I tried again, this time using Lore Segal's text. We did better, but we still never got out of Genesis.

It was, I had to acknowledge, not my native text, not one I could easily lead Anna through. We will probably try again sometime, and certainly we will hunt through it from time to time in search of answers to questions she is sure to ask in the future. But it seems ever more likely that her first big taste of the Bible will come, as it will for many of her generation, in a college literature course, juxtaposed with the Koran, the Bhagavad Gita, and the *Iliad*.

Chapter 5

IDENTITY

The religious scene was moving,
progressing all the time. What it lacked
was any kind of stability. It became
increasingly unlikely that an educated man
would support the cult of his parents, let
alone his grandparents; or even that he
would fail to change his cult once, perhaps
twice in his life. . . . Perhaps less noticeably,
the cults themselves were in constant osmosis.

—Paul Johnson, writing of the first
century B.C., in *A History of Christianity*

Two contradictory truths about religious identity in this country have long coexisted. On the one hand, ours is a country rooted in religious dissent and founded in a revolutionary claim of religious freedom. This was the one place on earth where one might choose one's own religion, without official penalty—and as often as might prove necessary to satisfy one's personal search for religious liberty and clarity.

On the other hand, as a nation checkered with rival religions and perspectives, religious affiliation early on came to serve as a sort of social calling card, an advertisement of class and attitudes that informed one's neighbors of much they might like to know before any deeper intimacy was attempted. From the beginning, a tension existed between the insularity of a community bound together by faith and shared rituals and the consciousness that another, alien, system of belief flourished down the street, in the next village over, or in a neighboring county or state. "An individual," John Dewey wrote of religion's historic role, "did not join a church—he was born and reared in a community whose social unity, organization and tradition were symbolized and celebrated in the rites, cults and beliefs of a collective religion." One's religion was the central ingredient in one's lineage—until the moment one decided to throw it over for a newer creed.

In *The Democratization of American Christianity*, Nathan Hatch examines this cycle of rebellion and conformity, of rejection and consolidation, through the prism of the "Second Great Awakening." Lasting from about 1800 to 1830, and coinciding with the rise of political populism in America, this period of intense religious revival turned the conventions of clerical authority inside out and gave birth to dozens of new denominations. At its core was both the conviction that every Christian was capable of finding God's truth for himself and a corresponding determination to seek it free of clerical direction. As the most fervent of the independent-minded preachers found it less and less tolerable to suffer the constraints of their learned sponsors, breakaway churches became the rule rather than the exception, their renegade leaders beholden to none and threatening to take off ever deeper into the thickets of personally interpreted Scripture. This fever of resolute individualism was captured in a poem attributed by dissenting Baptist preacher William Smythe Babcock of Springfield, Vermont, to an exceedingly precocious nine-year-old girl. Certainly the sentiments of the unnamed little sage corresponded to Babcock's own, as portrayed by Hatch, and he liked to quote her on his travels through New England in 1802 and 1803.

> Know then that every soul is free
> To choose his life and what he'll be;
> For this eternal truth giv'n,
> That God will force no man to heav'n.

He'll draw, persuade, direct him right;
Bless him with wisdom, love and light;
In nameless ways be good and kind,
But never force the human mind.

Competition for souls among rival denominations was intense, with much personal confusion resulting. Lucy Mack Smith, mother of Mormon founder Joseph Smith, and, like Babcock, a God-fearing child of the hill country of New Hampshire and Vermont, felt the dilemma keenly. "Lucy wrestled interminably with the problems of competing denominations," Hatch writes, "each of which seemed to invalidate the claims of the others. 'If I remain a member of no church,' she wrote, 'all religious people will say I am of the world; and if I join some one of the different denominations, all the rest will say I am in error.' After one disillusioning experience in a Presbyterian church, Lucy Smith returned home and came to the following conviction: 'I said in my heart that there was not then upon earth the religion which I sought.' "

In time, Lucy would find a minister who would agree to baptize her as a "solitary Christian," but the deep dissatisfaction she expressed in the available Christian creeds would ultimately find a more coherent voice in her son, who in founding his very own religion may have performed the quintessential American act.

Ours is a quieter religious era by far, but one that is also marked by discontent and by a spiritual wanderlust that is no longer confined to the Protestant majority. Catholics speak openly of progressive or conservative "factions" and observe a unofficial schism of belief and practice. Judaism is at one and the same time culturally resurgent and approaching extinction because of inter-marriage. An ever-increasing number of children, mean-while, bear hyphenated religious identities along with their hyphenated last names. Still, the question of what one actually believes has increasingly less to do with one's inherited religious identity than with a private and idio-syncratic mix of metaphysical "why nots" acquired from an unprecedented variety of sources. "I was not a be-liever," one woman told me in trying to explain how little her religious upbringing actually signified. "I was just someone who had been through Presbyterian Sunday school." While listening to two other women exchange religious histories one afternoon, one of them from a small town in California, the other from the Midwest, I was unable to keep track of the number of different de-nominations they had been affiliated with over the years. Though each experience had left some trace in their think-ing, and although both had decided to give their children some formal religious instruction, it was clear that no creed truly satisfied their personal search for meaning. What most animated them, rather, was the discovery that they had had nearly identical extrasensory contacts with their dead fathers—experiences that comforted them far more than conventional religion ever had, and which they took to be the most fundamentally spiritual experiences of their lives.

Where Lucy Mack Smith fretted over how her choice of a religion might be interpreted by others or serve to sever her from the larger community, the contemporary declaration of faith is far more likely to be addressed to the self, as part of an ongoing and private rumination. "This is my religion," one friend declares with a sweeping gesture that takes in both the October leaves falling from the sunlit trees and the strangers running or bicycling past as we circle the park. "I guess music is my religion," says another. Where one invests one's faith has come to depend less on a shared system of beliefs than on what most inspires the individual soul. "Sheilaism," Robert Bellah labeled such autonomous faith in *Habits of the Heart*, after a young woman named Sheila who located her belief in "my own little voice." By definition it is a religion of one.

And yet a large measure of what Lucy Mack Smith feared losing remains a perceived loss to the modern soul as well—the desire to belong, to be a member of some recognizable group, to be party to a coherent point of view, heir to a tradition. "In the community in which I grew up, outside Chicago," said Suzanne Trazoff, "*everybody* had a religion, except us. I can't tell you what a big deal was made in our family about our not being religious. Naturally, other people's religions appealed to me. I was sort of taken with whatever fell in my path, and I would go to church with whoever my best friend was at the time. I swore I would not do the same thing to my kids, but it turned out not to matter in their world the way it had in mine."

In the small town in northern California where my sister Katy and her husband, Jerry Early, are both teachers, religious affiliation still counts for a lot, and they have always known themselves and their son and daughter to be out of the ordinary in not belonging to a church. "Most of the people the kids know would identify themselves in terms of religion," said Katy. "It never mattered to Jake, because he never seemed to need the social verification, but it has been hard on Bridget. She went to the Presbyterian Sunday school with one friend on and off for about three years when she was younger. It was fine with me, and, in fact, I liked the idea of her getting some religious education. But she never liked the service and there was no real context, so she didn't learn very much. It had more to do with doing what her friends were doing, which is understandable in this community. I remember one of my students asking me what religion I was. I wanted to give her a proper answer but as a teacher I had to be careful. She was really hurt when I said I didn't go. I present a pretty conservative role model, and church is just assumed."

"I certainly always thought people needed it," said Jerry. "It was inculcated in me very early that 'good people go to church,' and, in fact, for most of my life, until a few years ago, I searched for a religion to call my own. It took me a long time to admit that I was an atheist. I've come to feel comfortable with what I think and what I believe, and I know that I'm a good person. Apart from disappointing Bridget, my only misgiving may be that I am excluded from a lot of groups because of it."

While religion's ability to define one's place in society or express a whole range of social attitudes has not altogether disappeared, it is greatly muted, particularly when one considers the rigid demarcations that used to exist. Anyone who came of age before the upheavals of the 1960s, for example, grew up in an America that was almost as sharply divided along religious lines as it was racially. Restrictive covenants barred Jews from the majority of suburban neighborhoods and clubs; the idea of a Catholic in the White House was anathema to the majority of non-Catholic voters; and an impressionable child could still tell her best friend, as Candace Burnett remembers being told a quarter century ago, that she could not sleep over on Saturday night for fear of endangering her "immortal soul" should the Congregational parents on duty fail to get her to mass the next morning.

It was a country in which a quiet but emphatic religious separatism prevailed among the three major religious groups—a "state of cold war" religion writer Peter Steinfels called it in a recent article in the *New York Times*. More often than not, as Dewey observed, one inherited one's religion and was bound by it. Not to live by its rules, not to observe its rituals, was to place oneself outside the community, and usually outside the family. Marriage to someone from an incompatible tradition was commonly looked upon as a disaster, with the greatest threat perceived across either of the yawning divides separating Christian and Jew, Catholic and Protestant.

Even beneath the broad umbrella of Protestantism, marriage between two distinct denominations tended to be tolerated only within accepted social boundaries, and so long as the doctrinal and ceremonial differences were not too dramatic. What passed for tolerable in one part of the country, moreover, was likely to be beyond the pale in another. "The worst thing I could have done was marry a Catholic," said Campbell Geeslin of growing up in a devoutly Methodist family in west Texas. "The next worst would have been a Baptist. I went with a friend to a Baptist church a few times when I was young, and it made my mother very uncomfortable. It was a matter of theology and class. Methodists are very orderly—they get their clergy the same way Episcopalians and Presbyterians do [assigned by the local bishop]. We thought of Baptists as sloppy—they get their own ministers, and their congregations break up over and over. I remember we wound up with three Baptist churches in this one little town."

Such fine distinctions would have been lost on the High Church Episcopalians of Muriel Hall's New Jersey childhood, who would have guarded against courting Methodists and Baptists with serene evenhandedness. "Of course, that would have been more social than theological," Hall recalls. "Presbyterians, on the other hand, presented a different sort of problem, because predestination, if the person took it seriously, would be a big problem for an Episcopalian. Also, in my day, the Episcopal Church would never let someone who was not confirmed receive Communion. So if you married someone who was a Unitarian, for example, you would be marrying someone who could never go to the Communion rail with you."

The social value of religious identity has never been a secret in this country, but its subtleties and permutations have tended to be invisible to those not within striking distance of dead center. The nose-thumbing acronym WASP, for example, while intended to describe the likes of George Bush, is so broadly constructed as to take in anyone from a Jehovah's Witness to a Four Square Baptist. But nobody means to poke fun at a Jehovah's Witness for lockjaw. They mean to poke fun at old-line Episcopalians, or, as Joseph Alsop explained in a 1989 essay, "The Wasp Ascendancy," the very small group of people

his forebears thought it "might be nice to know." Just
who was nice enough to know and who was not was
something religion helped define, not least for those "on
their way up in the world" and hoping to win admission
to the elite.

"If these [other Americans] rose far enough," Alsop
writes, "moreover, they had to be really pretty awful not
to be promptly absorbed into the WASP ascendancy.
Oddly enough, this absorption was then quite often ad-
vertised by ecclesiastical migration. My mother's family,
for example, was Scotch on her father's side, and basically
Dutch on the side of her mother, who was Theodore
Roosevelt's younger sister. Among the Scotch in my
mother's tribe, the migration began, despite howls of
Presbyterian rage from the primitive tribal majority,
when one of the tribe's leading males bought a pew in
Grace Church around 1840, 'because all the better people
go there. . . .'

"I do not know how soon thereafter my mother's family's Presbyterian to Episcopalian migration was com-
pleted or when the various branches of the Roosevelt clan
left their Dutch canticles. But all of them on both sides
certainly ended as Episcopalians. I fear, too, that the at-
traction of the Episcopal church lay in the simple fact that
this used to be almost everywhere the all-but-official
church of the WASP ascendancy. Pittsburgh was, and
perhaps is still, the exception that proves the rule. The
same ecclesiastical migration took place there, but Episcopalians were the ones who migrated, since the local
branch of the ascendancy remained firecely loyal to its
native Presbyterianism—and where Mellons went, there
went many more."

Alsop's amused tone reflects the distance from the heat of battle that time arranges, but the key terms in his account are "howls of rage" and "tribe." Even among those who didn't give a hoot for the creed printed in their prayer books, to change one's religion once meant something very like changing tribes, and the sense of betrayal and abandonment that resulted was genuine. Wounded or angry families routinely disowned errant sons and daughters, siblings boycotted one another's weddings, once-hopeful suitors and equally hopeful brides lived to regret contracts pledging to raise their future children in the other's religion. The children of such unions were often hit hard by the conflict that resulted. "My mother was a Protestant, my father a Catholic," says Sue O'Leary, one of six children born to parents who were never able to resolve the issue of which religion to raise them in. "She took us to Presbyterian Sunday school. He occasionally took us to mass—where we read *that* book [the Catholic Missal]. My mother was so against us being raised Catholic—and she got so much flak from his family for it. I grew up thinking religion was trouble."

In Jerry Delaney's family, a lifetime of religious sparring between his Catholic father and his Protestant mother culminated in a painful battle over where he and his sister would go to college. Having acquiesced in raising her children Catholic, Delaney's mother was set on her son going to Harvard, her daughter to Smith. With equal fervor, his father insisted on Georgetown and Manhattanville. "They fought tooth and nail," Delaney recalled years later, with a last-minute complication making it seem, briefly, as if his mother might win out in behalf of one of her children at least. "My sister had been awarded a partial scholarship by Manhattanville," Delaney remembers, "but then she got an even bigger one at Smith." While their mother took this as further evidence of Smith's greater suitability, their father—in the sort of scene that might have served as noble exhortation to generations of American Catholics struggling to reach the top of the heap without surrendering either their religious or ethnic identities—spurned the money differential and sent his daughter to Manhattanville, as planned. His son was dispatched to Georgetown, where he took his first tentative steps away from the church.

For successive immigrant populations, as for the sons and daughters of the Bible Belt, religious identity had even greater significance than for Joseph Alsop's forebears, in that it helped bind the group together against a common enemy, whether real or perceived. Expressions of anti-Catholicism and anti-Semitism were commonplace and unembarrassed, although simple ignorance of other religions was an equally effective segregator. Forbidden to so much as peek through the doors of a Protestant church or a synagogue, Catholic children worked themselves into frenzies of darkly imaginative anxiety about various "others." Indeed my own confusion about these matters as a small child was so intense that for years I mixed up the names Lucifer and Luther—equally popular Antichrists in the Catholic pantheon—and suffered nightmares after getting into a minor fight with a minister's son who lived a few blocks from us. Minister's son? The very idea was bound to cause nightmares for any properly raised Catholic child.

"Protestants were summer acquaintances," recalled Paul Fargis, summing up the practical effect of generations of parochial school isolation. And the ignorance was mutual. In *Mine Eyes Have Seen the Glory*, Randall Balmer tells of "witnessing" to a young neighbor he assumed, in his fundamentalist innocence, to have been in need of Christ. "Stanley," Balmer writes, "was a Roman Catholic, not a Christian, a plight in some respects worse than outright paganism . . . because it lulled followers into a deadly complacency. But *Christian*? Certainly no Catholic, no matter how benighted, would dare call himself a Christian."

We tell such stories on ourselves now from the perspective of a largely remade world, in which religious affiliation is only rarely an identifier capable of conveying more than a temporary message. Though the majority of Americans do, in fact, continue to describe themselves as members of one church or another, it is an identification that for most people trails behind job description, professional title, marital status, even geography. The choice of a church to belong to, meanwhile, is increasingly cut off from other life choices, including family or community tradition. Some 80 percent of American adults claim formal membership in a church, according to a 1991 survey by the California-based Barna Research Group, but only a third of these say they have belonged to the same church for twenty years or more. Almost as many report membership of five years or less—with 21 percent claiming even briefer association. Given that elderly members often claim seventy or eighty years in a congregation, the report notes, the overall average of seventeen years' membership in a church is misleading. It is probably much shorter.

"The environment for Christian affiliation in America

has changed," says George Barna, the president of the research firm. "It used to be that people who were baptized in one denomination probably would spend their whole lives in churches of that denomination. Today, someone who attended a church in one city, and moves to another city, won't necessarily limit their search for a church home to the denomination they came from. People are more open to changing churches today."

Barna himself is a perfect example. In *How to Find Your Church*, a manual for the perplexed which differs not a great deal from a car-buyer's guide (with chapters such as "What to Look For," "Hard to Get Information," "Figuring Out What a Church Believes," "Discerning Consumerism"), Barna describes how he and his wife went through five such searches in a few years' time. "Without any idea of what [they] stood for, how they differed, or what to expect, we went to Catholic, Presbyterian, Baptist and non-denominational churches," Barna writes of their first shopping expedition. Subsequent moves to distant parts of the country forced them to repeat the process several times over. "Six months and thirteen churches later," he writes of one year's search; "Six months and another fourteen churches," he writes of a second. Having settled finally into a Presbyterian congregation in Glendale, California, Barna, a one-time advertising man whose clients include the Disney empire and a variety of "Christian and secular" organizations, has plenty of advice to offer churches hoping to survive into the next millennium in a tough market. In addition to providing basic statistical data, his group markets a line of pamphlets with titles like "User-Friendly Churches," "Marketing the Church" and "Never on a Sunday: The Challenge of the Unchurched," which outline strategies for attracting new members or revitalizing a lukewarm congregation—from unannounced visits to a potential member's home (likely to backfire) and telemarketing (lots of negative fallout there, too) to sponsorship of a seminar or cultural event (best bet). In the world Barna addresses, religious affiliation is totally up for grabs, and he betrays genuine astonishment at the survival of tradition as a factor in choosing one's church.

"Amazingly," he writes in *We Have Seen the Future: The Demise of Christianity in Los Angeles County*, "the majority of the people have apparently selected their church on the basis of factors that have little to do with the actual content or personality of the church. By far the most influential reason for church selection was family tradition: having been raised in the church, having been brought up in churches within that denomination, the desire to please parents by attending the same church, etc. More than half the adults in the county attend their current church due to such a reason. This reasoning was especially common among Catholics and the elderly."

That a sense of connection to the past as an influence on one's choice of a church could be seen as anachronistic rather than unremarkable suggests how greatly our expectations about religious identity have changed. In fact, people switch congregations or denominations for important reasons and trivial ones, after long reflection and none at all. For some, it is undoubtedly part of a search for deeper meaning, greater spiritual clarity, or a more appealing aesthetic—the modern equivalent of Lucy Mack Smith's struggle to find the one true church. For as many others, probably, it has less to do with theology, church politics, or ideology than with the ingrained national habit of moving on, for the sake of a new job or the hope of starting over. And in some cases, it is itself the continuation of a long tradition.

In an account similar to many I heard, Jim O'Leary recalled how in moving around the state of Ohio, his family first attended "a Lutheran church, then a Congregational, then a Presbyterian. It was," he said, "more a case of 'pick your sermon' if you cared enough, otherwise you just usually went to the closest church." As an adult searching for a place to take his son, O'Leary did as he had been taught, and wound up in yet another denomination—for a time. After teaching Sunday school in a Dutch Reform church for three years, a professional move to another city sent him looking, once the family was settled, for another church to join. He found it at the end of the block.

If O'Leary's experience represents denominational indifference, Sue Gilger's decision to join the Episcopalian Church a decade after fleeing her rural Baptist upbringing represents the opposite: a deeply considered shift of spiritual allegiance. "Until I was a teenager," Gilger recalls, "my life was completely church, yet I always felt myself to be lacking somehow. We were told that everything in the Bible was true—a strict, literal interpretation. Whenever I asked questions," she says, "I was given pat answers." Partially in rebellion, she married young and swore she would never go back to church. "Even after the kids were born, I didn't go back right away," she says, but eventually relented when she realized how much she wanted her children to know the Bible stories and moral lessons she had absorbed as a child, "things that were second nature to me but which I didn't have the ability to teach." Because her husband, John, had grown up Episcopalian, they chose a local Episcopal church, where she unexpectedly discovered a true community and a reborn faith. Though the impetus had been her children, "it opened up a whole new life for me, a sense of my own spirituality. I think of it," she says, "as going from an elementary school education to a college understanding."

As a rule, the degree of alienation from one's original denomination, or reengagement in a new one, is typically less dramatic that Sue Gilger's, the investment in a particular church more lasting than Jim O'Leary's, and the solution for each to be had in a less radical move—to the church down the block or across town, where the minister knows how to tell a better story or a quicker one, where the Sunday school is better organized or the interpretation of the Gospels a better fit to one's economic circumstances or political conscience. In America, there is always an alternative, always a greener pasture—in religion as in everything else.

Leading the pack in this instance, as in so many other societal changes, is the huge baby-boom generation. In their 1989 study of the baby-boomers' relationship to organized religion, Wade Clark Roof and David A. Roozen describe an abrupt increase in formal affiliation as a result of the aging of this forever-young group and of their unusually delayed status as parents. But their report stresses the fact that this generation's involvement "appears . . . to be on different terms than for previous generations. While previous generations generally took their religious commitments and participation for granted, it appears that baby-boomers approach these more as a calculated choice, one which consciously involves discriminating decisions between various religious alternatives, including of course the option of no participation . . . at all. Choice in matters of faith and practice is as much taken for granted for this generation as were expectations of religious involvement for previous generations."

"Members of this generation," they conclude, "move freely 'into' and 'out of' religious institutions, in what has to be seen as an open religious environment. . . . It is probably the case that no recent American generation exhibits as much religious and spiritual fluidity as this one."

While it is tempting to read into such transience a somewhat fundamental skimpiness of faith, it is not so much that the religiously peripatetic believe nothing, but that the received truths that have long constituted "belief," and especially those espoused by the mainstream churches, are themselves changing so rapidly and unpredictably as to oblige the individual to continually reinvent—or re-ally—himself religiously.

"Before World War II," explains Daniel Aleshire, associate director of the Association of Theological Schools, "there were, in fact, greater distinctions between religious groups. The downside to it was that there was more suspicion, but the positive side was that Methodists tended to stay Methodist, Baptists, Baptist, Presbyterians, Presbyterian. Now, by contrast, when people move to a new place, they seek to find a church to suit certain needs and it may happen that it is a church of another denomination. If they had stayed in their hometowns, they probably would have stayed in their original denominations as well."

One of the many consequences of this unsettled religiosity has been a weakening of tradition within all the major religious bodies, a phenomenon cited repeatedly in a 1989 piece in the *New York Times* on the shortage of impressive seminary candidates. In addition to a marked increase in the age of applicants and a broad concern that many candidates have turned to the ministry only after unsuccessful attempts at careers elsewhere, the article noted a "difference between today's seminarians and their predecessors [that] appears to be true regardless of faith or denomination, gender or age: They are less grounded in their own religious tradition."

Whereas in 1966, 95 percent of entering Catholic seminarians had attended Catholic college, and 70 to 80 percent had attended Catholic elementary or high schools, just over 50 percent of the current crop had attended Catholic college and even fewer had been exclusively educated in parochial schools. A similarly dramatic dilution has taken place among Jews and Protestants. "The big difference," said a representative of a national Jewish organization, "is that the Judaic and Hebrew background of the current applicants is much weaker." Likewise, Daniel Aleshire, at the time director of professional studies at Southern Baptist Seminary, reported that only half of that institution's current enrollees were graduates of Baptist colleges. "You can no longer assume a common background," observed Aleshire. "People entering seminary haven't absorbed the cultural patterns, the inarticulated systems that are alive in any denomination."

In *Culture Wars*, author James Davison Hunter attempts to organize the chaos of convictions that currently characterize American religious life into a dualist division between "progressive" and "orthodox" factions within each of the major religious bodies. In addition to claiming power for their respective viewpoints within their own denominations, Hunter argues, the two sides are seeking to define the moral culture of the nation through a set of social issues that include abortion, prayer in the schools, sex education, the rights of homosexuals, public support of the arts, and so on. "Politics," he writes, "is, in large part, an expression of culture. . . . At the heart of culture, though, is religion, or systems of faith. And at the heart of religion are its claims to truth about the world. This is it in a nutshell."

Hunter makes a strong case for his image of a divided national morality. There are, indeed, powerful conservative and liberal constituencies within Protestantism, Catholicism, and Judaism in America, and they do at times appear to have more in common with one another than with their respective flocks. But such a schema tends to oversimplify the free-for-all that has succeeded the old order. There are not two cleanly defined positions in competition but a cacophony of "truths." Just as the traditional Republican and Democratic party ideologies no longer seem adequate to represent the spectrum of American political thinking, or the concerns of its citizens, the long-standing conceit that America is a unified moral entity no longer persuades. What is striking is how readily this splintered vision throws up new churches and new "moral alliances" devoted to social issues—the Moral Majority, James Dobson's Focus on the Family, and the antiabortion organization Operation Rescue being among the best known on the right side of the political spectrum, with Norman Lear's People for the American Way holding forth for the left—and how unsuccessful are comparable efforts to create even a third political party.

"I think Americans are more passionate about religion than they are about politics," says Randall Balmer. "If you compare us to Europe, it's interesting to see how they have hundreds of political parties compared to our two very centrist parties, one or two religions compared to our thousands of different denominations. I think we somehow syphon our social discontent away from politics into religion. People who are dissatisfied with the status quo tend to exhibit it in terms of religion rather than politics. In Europe, religion is utterly at the margin of society. But religion in America is populist, and the religious entrepreneurs are all out there, each one trying to be more popular than the next."

Except that *passionate* is by far too intense a word to describe the religious feelings of most of the nonevangelical majority, Balmer's reading of the relationship between religion and politics captures a significant truth. In the same way that Americans unhappy with their economic or social lot in one part of the country are far more likely to uproot themselves and their children and move somewhere new than to become involved with any effort to change local conditions, so are they far readier to replace an old religious identity with a new one. It would not be unjust to say they practice a sort of denominational serial monogamy.

But while greater mobility certainly accounts for some degree of denomination switching at the grassroots level, the phenomenon has also been fed by philosophical ex-

hortation from the top down. "Post–World War II," says
Daniel Aleshire, "we had twenty-five or thirty years of
a strong ecumenical movement among Protestants. Most
of the unions that were talked about never came about,
but you had all those years in which the formal position
of most churches was that the idea of Christianity as a
whole was more important than individual denominations. We taught a whole generation not to value denominations. Vatican II brought many of the same kinds of
changes to Catholics—the idea that Protestants might not
be quite as evil as once thought. Intermarriage, of course,
took it another step. Now that the Methodist has married
the Episcopalian, what are they going to do about the
kids? For many, the solution is a looser affiliation with
either."

In fact, probably no single factor has had quite the
impact on religious identity in the last quarter century as
marriage between members of different faiths. What was
once the alarming exception has become a virtual commonplace, while the attitude most people bring to it has
dramatically changed. The sort of interdenominational
squabbling that so often characterized the "mixed" marriage of past generations is increasingly hard to imagine
in our postecumenical age. Religion has become one of
the things we pass along to our children only if we choose
to. It is, as one mother remarked, no longer a given in
life but "an elective." One gets married in a church or a
temple—or one doesn't; one baptizes one's children or
arranges a bris—or one doesn't. And still one is invited
to dinner by the in-laws—where the number of denominations represented at table is likely to be limited only
by the number of siblings and their spouses. Superficially,

at least, it seems as if the choice is of little consequence. Contemporary unions abound in religious Romeos and Juliets—and only rarely do their elders raise an objection.

Believing the issue to be minor, partners in a mixed marriage are often caught up short by the discovery that seemingly small differences have a long reach. The sudden juxtaposition of another point of view, another philosophy, is jarring enough for some married couples. The realization that you are dealing with your partner's deeply rooted religious convictions, as well as your own, can be truly unnerving. "He believes in original sin," a friend announced one day, as if she had just figured out the answer to everything confounding about her husband. Even for parents who are not religiously inclined, it can come as something of a surprise when stirrings of religious proprietariness surface, or when differences of style or custom are suddenly seen as having their base in an identity one imagined one no longer cared about. "I never thought we would argue about something like this," said one young mother, who was surprised to discover that she did, in fact, care whether her infant daughter would be baptized in her church or her husband's. It was not a matter of doctrine or dogma, but of familiarity, of remaining on familiar territory.

"Sometimes," another woman reflected, "it occurs to me with a real start that my daughter is 'half Jewish,' and I have this weird sequence of thoughts: Oh, no, because *I'm* not Jewish, she isn't technically, either—as if I'm somehow passing on to her genetically the essence of being a Christian—or do I really mean WASP here? Physically she looks so much like her father, which pleases me, but in other ways she is like me, and like someone from my background, and I want that to count as well. It isn't religion so much as an identity that goes very far back."

It is much that same sense of wanting to insure a connection of some sort that prompts parents to baptize or confirm their children in religions they no longer practice, or never did. Some do it to link their children to a distant culture, as Kaari Ward's parents did in confirming her in the Russian Orthodox Church; others to honor long-dead relatives. Several nonreligious parents told of baptizing their adopted children in an attempt to tie them symbolically to birth parents who were religious, and one thoroughly secular young man told me of his astonishment when his equally secular adoptive parents confessed an unkept pledge to raise him as an orthodox Jew. It was a message about identity that he simply did not know how to interpret—like news of a landless title from a country one never expects to visit.

For some, how seriously one takes the issue of religious identity turns out, unsurprisingly, to depend on how close to the altar or the delivery room one is. When Fred Herschkowitz and Jean Kunhardt first met, he had not been in a synagogue for thirty years except as his widowed father's occasional companion, and she, despite coming from an Episcopalian family with a grandfather and a brother in the priesthood, had given equally little thought to the question of religious identity. "I'd never met an Episcopalian," Fred said. "I didn't know what they were. Well, I knew they were president a lot, or had country clubs and said, 'Hi, Bob!' a lot. 'How's Betty?' But you know, we fell in love and religion wasn't important then. I felt accepted by her family, and my father, who had actually not liked a lot of my girlfriends, adored Jean. He liked her family, too, so it was like his blessing. It didn't trouble him that Jean's brother married us, that we didn't have a rabbi."

But Philip Kunhardt, Jean's brother, had also given them a book on interfaith marriage, and Fred started thinking more seriously about what it meant to be a Jew. "I had a very lazy way of being a Jew when I was a kid. I always had a sense of who I was, but it wasn't in religious terms. Once I started thinking about having kids, it made a big difference. Jean and I began talking about it, and though we agreed it was a good idea, we really didn't have any idea of what we were getting into at the start. Jean started asking me all these questions about being a Jew—what this meant, what that meant, what's this holiday, what are the roots of this? And I had to say I couldn't answer a lot of her questions."

"I'm not particularly religious," Jean had said a couple of years earlier, when their daughter, Eliza, was a year old, "and though I feel there is a God, I don't feel much of a need to observe. What I do love is the concept of belonging to a community with a coherent philosophy, with fixed holidays, and a particular way of looking at things. Judaism has never seemed at all alien to me, and so in the beginning it seemed like an easy thing to do. Now, I still feel I want to do it, but it comes with a much heavier heart." By this time, she and Fred had begun attending something called "learner's minyan" at a nearby synagogue on Saturday mornings, and though it was very exciting to them both, it had helped Jean see how big a commitment was involved. She was not interested in doing it casually, in being one of those people who toss off a seder as if it were some sort of "theme" dinner party. As a result, she said, "I've begun to see what I have to give up if I want to do this right. It sort of embarrasses me, but I have to say that when I think of Christmas—well, you know how people say they hate it when their babies wake up at night? I loved it, and every time I would hear Eliza cry and I would get up and nurse her I would say to Fred, 'It's just like Christmas.' Because my parents made it so special for us. And the thought of not being able to give that tradition to Eliza is very painful to me."

At the same time, she said, there was no doubt in her mind that it was the right way to go. "I really don't believe it's easy or desirable to do both, to have two religions. I think you need to choose, so the kid won't be all at sea. I want Eliza to grow up with a solid sense of who she is," she continued, "but the little I've learned so far has made me realize that I'm still an outsider—and as an outsider I can't give that to her fully. I need to know more, so I can do this wholeheartedly."

Over the next few years, she and Fred continued to attend the learner's minyan together, while gradually becoming more involved in the life of the synagogue, attending cultural events and Hanukkah and Purim celebrations. When Eliza was four, and her sister Suzannah had just been born, they started taking her to a children's minyan as well. "The teacher explains traditions and customs and language," says Fred. "She throws in a Hebrew word once in a while, and she talks about some of the myths and the fables and the Bible and the Torah. We love it."

Passover and Hanukkah were spent with Jean's partner

and her husband, a rabbi. Christmas was spent with Jean's large family, ankle deep in wrapping paper and cousins, and lit by the glow of an enormous Christmas tree. They no longer put up a tree at their own house, a decision that Jean had made, but there was no shortage of celebration. "I'm always amazed by how quickly kids get invested in these joy holidays," Jean had observed earlier, and now she could see how her own daughters were acquiring customs as natural to them as her family's had been to her. Whether Jean would ever formally convert remained open, but she was clear on what she wanted for her daughters. Originally, she and Fred had assumed that as the children of a non-Jewish mother, the girls would not technically become Jewish until they were bat mitzvahed in adolescence. But at some point, Rachel Cowan, their rabbi, herself an adult convert, mentioned the tradition of the mikvah, or ritual bath, and they liked the idea. Like Christian baptism, it would be a clarifying symbol, formally marking the girls as members of a community.

Suzannah was too young to understand, but Fred and Jean explained to Eliza that they were going to have a special ceremony for her and her sister to celebrate being Jewish, and because Jean wasn't born Jewish, this would mark its importance for them in a special way. Fred joked a lot about how the girls were "going under" and Jean thought about little else. Plans for the service were finally made, and one morning in the spring of 1992, Fred and Jean, Eliza, Suzannah, and Rachel Cowan made their way to a brownstone in the neighborhood that discreetly houses a mikvah. "It was like walking into a beautiful little spa," Jean said afterward. "There were two other rabbis there, and one of them gave a very sweet talk, and then they questioned me in great detail about why I wanted to do this, and what it meant to me. They obviously wanted to make sure I was not being coerced. And then Fred picked up both the girls—they had to have nothing on, not even a bit of nail polish, and Eliza had a little streak of green Magic Marker on her that we had to clean off first—and then Fred just took them down the steps into this pool and he said the prayer that Jews say for anything 'new and special,' and dunked them under. It was very joyous, with lots of *mazel tovs*. And Rachel talked to them after and said, 'Well, of course, you were Jewish before, because your daddy is Jewish, but now you're really Jewish!'

"Then I had to go off to work and Rachel and I walked out together. I had been feeling very emotional about this event for weeks ahead of time, wondering whether this was the right thing to do, thinking about nothing else, and I had talked to Rachel about it many times. And now she turned to me and said, 'How do you feel?' And I said, 'I feel great.' And it was so true. And it's a feeling that has lasted. At the same time, my sense that this is a complicated thing has grown over the years. When I first decided it was important to raise the girls Jewish, I felt very clear, almost dogmatic, about choosing the one tradition and wiping out the other. Now I see it as a lifelong journey, and I see also that you only choose for your children for a time. Later on, they choose for themselves. But for me, I'm grateful. If I hadn't married someone who was Jewish, I don't think I ever would have thought about any of this at all, and I would have missed something wonderful."

The difficulty of remaking one's religious identity, and, for children, the ultimately arbitrary nature of whatever choice is made in their behalf, should not be underestimated, as was rather differently illustrated a few years ago by the case of a divorced couple in Colorado. The husband in this case was, like Fred Herschkowitz, Jewish, the wife a Catholic who had converted to Judaism at the time of the marriage. After several years and the birth of two daughters, the parents were divorced. The wife was awarded custody of the girls, who by that time had begun attending Hebrew school, and presumably thought of themselves as Jewish. Soon after the divorce, however, the mother reconsidered her earlier conversion, returned to Catholicism, and eventually married a Catholic. While continuing to take her daughters to Hebrew school on Saturday, she also began taking them to mass on Sunday, claiming the girls were entitled to be exposed to both faiths. The father didn't see it that way and sued for the exclusive right to determine his children's religious training. As his lawyer put it in a newspaper interview, "Either Jesus is the Messiah or he is not."

The court, of course, was neither obliged nor empowered to rule on the implicit theological dispute, only on the enforceability of the wife's promise to raise any children as Jews. A court-appointed evaluator recommended that custody not be split, but the judge sided with the father on contractual grounds, a decision that survived the mother's appeal and included a charge of contempt (later dropped) against the mother for taking the children to mass.

Reading of this dispute in the paper, I found myself sympathetic to both parents—each of whom quite understandably wanted the children to identify with himself, or herself, religiously. But I couldn't help but side with the father on logical grounds; that is, it seemed to me impossible to raise children in two faiths simultaneously, at least not if you mean for them to take you, or belief, seriously. As the lawyer so bluntly summarized, either Jesus was the Messiah or he wasn't.

The issue seemed so obvious to me that I assumed most people, however sympathetic, would agree. The children could learn about both faiths, certainly, and be raised to respect them both, but they could not *be* both. When I mentioned the case to a number of friends and interview subjects, however, the most common reaction was, Why not? Because Judaism declares the Messiah yet to come, while Christianity claims he has already arrived, I said. Because Jews reject the idea that God "became man," while the divinity of Christ and his redemptive sacrifice form the core of Christian belief. But there's nothing wrong with giving children both points of view, I was told. That's not the same as raising a child in a particular faith, I replied. You're taking too narrow a perspective, I was told.

In other words, to a fair number of people, the particulars of a given creed—even its most central tenets— weighed less than the concept of "equal time" for the religion of each parent. "When I was growing up," Fred Herschkowitz said about his and his wife's decision, "you couldn't be a Giant and a Dodger fan. You had to choose. But a lot of people who heard I got married kept trying to say something they thought would sound nice—'It's great,' they'd say, 'the kids will have Easter *and* Passover, Christmas *and* Hanukkah.' I guess they say it because they don't know what else to say—like 'What's he *doing*?' "

It's hard to know which choice prompts the question most often. No less a figure than Harvey Cox, Harvard Divinity School professor and author of *The Secular City*, has publicly made the case in favor of the plausibility of a dual religious identity. Cox's second marriage, in 1986, to a Jewish professor of Russian history, made him the father of a child destined to be bar mitzvahed just before the close of the century—not a first for a Baptist minister, I would venture, but hardly as common as it is among the nonclerical classes. In an interview in the *New York Times Magazine* in May 1988, Cox attempted to make sense of this interesting tangle.

"Nina and I went for counseling to Rabbi Louis Mintz," Cox told writer Dan Wakefield, "and I told him, 'I know that Jewish law says the child of a Jewish woman is Jewish and he should be raised Jewish and I think it is right. The only thing I insist on is I want to help raise him Jewish.' Rabbi Mintz was pleased, but said, 'Of course, at some point your child will say, "Hey, I understand you're one of the best known Protestant theologians." How will you deal with that?' I said, 'When the times comes.'

"I think," Cox continued, "we're in a stage now in the relationship between Jews and Christians in which a child can grow up being part of both these traditions without violating either one. He'll be raised Jewish and he'll get the 'Christian addendum' to the Jewish story—that's what it really is, a 'postcript,' saying 'Look, we're a part of this, too.' "

A few weeks later, the magazine published a letter from a rabbi in Pennsylvania who offered a slightly more acid

interpretation. "I am stunned that one of the world's fore-
most theologians would suggest that a child can grow up
in both Jewish and Christian traditions and not violate
either one," wrote Rabbi Jeffrey Salkin. "More disturbing
is Harvey Cox's suggestion that his child would be raised
Jewish but would get the 'Christian addendum' to the
Jewish story. Is he saying that this addendum is necessary
for the fulfillment of Judiasm? To these ears, it sounds
like the old Christian triumphalism that supposedly was
going out of style."

However untenable Cox's position is theologically, it
is also, given his personal, and increasingly common,
circumstances, emotionally understandable. Nobody
wants to be forced to surrender the tradition that nour-
ished him from infancy, and who, least of all an ecu-
menically minded Cambridge Baptist, wants to demand
such a sacrifice of the beloved? In the preecumenical age,
such sacrifices were the common, and seemingly necessary, solution to intractable circumstances; confronted by
the institutional immutability of the Catholic church, of
Orthodox Judaism, or of one's fervently Protestant family, something—or someone—had to give. One could
not have it both ways. Today, having it both ways is what
one is entitled to; neither party feels obliged to jump ship;
neither is prepared to demand such a defection of the
other. Fairness, therefore, demands that the institutions
bend, not the star-crossed lovers.

After all, runs the principle counterargument to any
claim for denominational exclusivity, organized religion
is just a form given to the desire to believe, or the fact
of belief, and forms are arbitrary and changeable, just as
rules are. What counts is imparting a sense of the sacred

to children, of teaching them that something greater than oneself exists. And that can be done by one religion as well as another.

The last part of the argument—that a sense of the sacred, and the ineffable, can be reached as readily through one religion as another—is a claim I find hard to dismiss personally. But if it really makes no difference, what exactly is being held out for so powerfully?

In fact, I think the issue has very little to do with theology and everything to do with loyalty and a peculiarly American form of the heraldic impulse, much like the generational taste for compound surnames. Every influence gets credit—a natural enough urge as we observe ourselves melting in the national pot—but amounting, in religious terms, to fantasy. One may be, by birth, part English, Irish, African-American, and Hungarian, but one is not also by birth therefore Anglican, Roman Catholic, Baptist, and Jewish. One must choose, or be chosen for, or else one is talking about the past only. Which is something that a great many people who are no longer seriously religious are yet reluctant to acknowledge—in some cases, probably for simple lack of linguistic imagination, in others, from a reluctance to concede the hollowness of a tradition that survives in name only.

Of the many people I interviewed who profess belief in a nontrinitarian Supreme Being, for example, only one made use of the simple and essentially unimprovable term "deist" to describe her current position. As the carefully schooled daughter of an Episcopalian priest, this woman is perhaps unusually disinclined to misuse a theological term for convenience's sake; yet it is not pedantry that leads her to the once-familiar phrase but frankness, as well as a long-standing affection for America's best known deist, Thomas Jefferson. Having abandoned the fundamental doctrine of Christ's divinity in her youth, she no longer considers herself an Episcopalian, nor even a Christian. Those terms correctly describe what she *was*. "Deist" describes what she believes herself to be.

Naming oneself religiously, and naming one's children, seems to be a particular necessity in America. It is hard to get away from it, even if one tries. "There are things that stop you cold," said Jonina Herter, "like when Norman went into the army and they asked, 'What religion are you?' and he wasn't allowed to say, 'None.' It's the same thing with Noah's camp. I can't say, 'None,' on the form, but 'None' is what my children have been given."

> Once a Catholic, always a Catholic.
>
> —old Protestant saying

It was not until I was twenty-one and had left home that I properly understood what was obvious to everyone else—that before I was anything else in the world's eyes, I was Irish-Catholic. I say that it was obvious, but in reality, since neither my name nor my appearance was conspicuously Irish, it generally took a minute or two of conversation for strangers to discover the fact, a little longer for me to take in how significant they found it. A query about where I had gone to school was usually sufficient, and in the amazed responses that the answer prompted—"Immaculate WHAT?" and the succeeding series of slack-jawed comments (*How* many brothers and sisters? Two of them *nuns?*), I decided that the wider world I had joined was at least as parochial and attached to clan tags as the Catholic world I had recently left. It was my first lesson in the significance of religious identity.

As it happened, I came of age at an unprecedented moment for American Catholics, in which the simultaneous ascensions to power of the unexpectedly revolutionary Pope John XXIII and the Harvard-educated John F. Kennedy made it not only acceptable to be Catholic, but interesting and enviable—even, for the first time since the Reformation, intellectually enviable. For someone who had attended Catholic schools for eighteen years, from nursery school through college, this turn of events proved the social equivalent of an amnesty, sparing me for a time the discovery that *my* intellectual life and the nation's were not a match. It was simply not necessary for me to take notice, as my parents, or even my older siblings, had been obliged to. My brother, an unhappy graduate of Notre Dame, had once astonished me by saying he had always felt vaguely "un-American" as a Catholic. I, on the other hand, had grown to adulthood without ever having to relinquish that most sublime illusion of childhood—that one's self, wrapped in the tender batting of one's perfect family, inhabits the true center of the universe, all its ways the right ways, all its customs eternal.

As time went by and I continued to separate what I deeply valued in my upbringing from what I rejected, I found myself referring to myself not as an ex-Catholic, with its overtones of formal renunciation, but as someone who had "grown up Catholic," a locution that, while it did not express my complicated position fully, at least did not misrepresent it. I wanted, clearly, to be understood to have come from somewhere, to have a context, and that context was unalterably Catholic.

By the time my daughter was born, that context had been supplanted by a far less easily defined and more idiosyncratic one, in which having been a Catholic seemed to matter less each year—much less, it seemed to me, than the fact of having grown up in my particular family, born to my particular parents, raised in the particular places I was raised, at a particular time in history. My having been a Catholic began to seem more like an accident of birth than a foreordained certainty, with my more recent history quite literally superseding earlier memories. It was as if I had been born in some distant country, and the longer I went without a return visit, the more I came to disbelieve its reality. Yet both independently and as the object of others' insistence, I found such a radical dissociation almost equally hard to believe. Where had it gone? How could it have gone so completely? What had I replaced it with?

On those infrequent occasions when I visited a church for a funeral or a wedding, I half-expected to be seduced back—if not to faith, then to allegiance, or alliance. More often, I felt like an anthropologist with an in. I knew all the customs, could anticipate every gesture. And even though I might be moved to tears by the sound of un-coached voices straining to reach the high notes of "Holy God We Praise Thy Name," I always came away thinking not about reentering this world of my childhood but of how unbreachably remote it now seemed. Whatever at-tachment I felt was prompted not by the rituals of the church but by the residual affection I felt for the sort of people I had grown up among and the quality of calm and certitude that being part of such a community makes possible. I did not miss being in church, yet I found I did miss being with the kind of exurban Irish and Italians I would long ago have sat next to there and whom I seldom encountered in adult life.

Standing on Fifth Avenue to watch the St. Patrick's Day parade for the first time in that same period, I remember being absolutely overwhelmed by the sight of so many faces out of my childhood, and by a sense of connection I hadn't expected to feel. Every altar boy I'd ever known seemed reincarnate here as a beefy cop or limber fireman, marching up the avenue in squadron formation, short-skirted cheerleaders following hard behind with green pom-poms waving, family after blue-eyed family smiling from the curb. Like an expatriate reduced to tears by an unexpected sighting of the flag, I wanted both to stand aloof and to be counted in.

Yet when push came to shove, which is to say, when I became a parent, it was suddenly no longer confusing in any real sense at all. Despite the sentimental tugs I felt, and continue to feel, despite the flooding memories of white dresses and sweet-smelling flowers, despite a persistent, if erratic, admiration for many things Catholic, I was no longer a Catholic and could not make myself into one again. I was an ex-Catholic, a different species altogether, and that is who my daughter would have for a mother.

For many Catholics I know personally, and many others I talked to for this book, it is a familiar story. Ex-Catholics form a small universe, subdivided into nation-states of the bitter, the joyful, and the sorrowful. Most of us, given our numbers, can claim a sibling or two in each of them, as well as among the continuing "body of the faithful." In my family, the lineup includes two ex-nuns, one of them married to an ex-priest, the other to a divorced

Protestant; a brother who currently works, and actually lives, in a Lutheran church; another who once tried to hire lawyer Melvin Belli in hopes of suing the Church for damages. Two of us took up with hereditary Episcopalians, and two others married converts from Protestantism. Of eight siblings, the only one of us who fulfilled expectations by marrying an Irish-Catholic of similar background had her four closely spaced children baptized one after another and then quit the Church for good.

As catalogues go, ours is unexceptional. Virtually every Catholic I spoke to gave a similar variety-pack accounting: the sister in a cult, the brother in an ashram, two out of six sending their kids to religion class, three out of five living out of wedlock, two divorced, one just mikvahed, and the last of the faithful trying to decide whether to have a tubal ligation—her priest, it turns out, recommends it.

The last twenty-five years have been hard going for *the* Church, as Catholics liked to call it. ("The only *the* Church," as Gary Wills quotes Lenny Bruce's left-handed compliment.) Anyone taking bets on its future through the 1970s and '80s, as the convents and the rectories emptied out and the parochial schools shut down, might well have guessed it would all be over by the end of the century. Lots of people argue that it already is. All the visible marks of its unchangingness, of its distinctiveness, seem to have been jettisoned, in a wild splurge joined in by clergy and faithful. No more Latin, no more fish on Friday, no more confession boxes, no more fasts before Communion, no more extorting pledges from non-Catholics daring to marry into the tribe. Also no more

Saint Christopher medals, no more limbo, and who knows—maybe even no more bingo. In their place there is the Saturday night mass option, the rite of reconciliation, Confraternity of Christian Doctrine class and, in the dwindling number of Catholic schools that survive, near-majorities of eager, disciplined, non-Catholic students.

Most of all, there is freedom of conscience, and for Catholics who grew up under the old dispensation, that is the most shocking difference of all. At one time, what most characterized a Catholic, for Catholics and non-Catholics alike, was obedience to acknowledged authority; today it is the personal decision to remain one.

A few years ago, Anna Quindlen wrote a column for the *New York Times* in which she told the story of having lunch with a ninety-year-old priest at a nursing home, who, on learning how old she was, "said with some satisfaction, 'You were a Catholic when being a Catholic still meant something.'

"What does it mean now?" Quindlen went on to ask. "For myself, I cannot truly say. Since the issue became material to me, I have not followed the church's teaching on birth control. I disagree with its stand on abortion. I believe its resistance to the ordination of women priests is a manifestation of a mysogyny that has been with us longer than the church has. Yet it would never have occurred to my husband or me not to be married in a Catholic church, not to have our children baptized. On hospital forms and in political polls, while others leave the space blank or say 'none of your business,' I have no hesitation about giving my religion.

"We are cultural Catholics," she wrote, whose "Catholicism is . . . now not so much a system of beliefs or a set of laws but a shared history. It is not so much our faith as our past."

"To a certain extent," she elaborated when I spoke with her a year or so later, "being Catholic is what we *are*. I am Irish and I am Italian. I feel the same way about being a Catholic. When I tell my kids about my childhood, if I left out the Catholic part, they would only be getting 60 percent of the story.

"When we were in college," she said, "we let it drop like everybody else. We went to mass when we were at home. We went to midnight mass as a social event. That went on through our twenties, with most of our church attendance having to do with critical events in our lives or our families' lives—funerals, a few baptisms, not many weddings. But when we had kids, we knew we were going to have them baptized, we knew they were going to be part of a long line of Irish-Italian Catholics."

In fact, because of the changes that have occurred since Quindlen's childhood and the open differences she has with the Church on so many issues, the chances of her children getting anything like 60 percent of "the Catholic part" of her and her husband's story are slight. What she is talking about transmitting to them is a greatly altered version of what it means to be a Catholic—one considerably improved in the opinion of the majority of modern Catholics I've interviewed, but different in far greater degree than anything that distinguished Quindlen's own childhood experience from that of her parents'. For one thing, though she may count herself a Catholic by tradition, it is, as she makes clear in a separate essay, a matter of choice and self-definition in a way that simply was not possible for previous generations.

"I would have a real problem raising my kids Catholic if I were an agnostic or an atheist," Quindlen says. "And if I had to regurgitate the letter of the law, it would be much harder. But I feel comfortable with the New Testament and with the example of the Parables, which philosophically communicates so much of what I want to give them anyway."

If Quindlen's precise views on a given range of issues cannot be presumed to be representative of the majority of Catholics of her generation, or any other, her sense of entitlement to a point of view most certainly is. Made confident by the changes that grew out of the second Vatican Council—and especially by such documents as *Dignitatis Humanae*, which argued in favor of the individual conscience—modern Catholics enjoy a freedom that would have been unimaginable to their parents' generation. Of my seven siblings, only two remain practicing Catholics, and only one of them continues to operate within a largely Catholic world. Even within that world, everything is different, she says. "No one I know is a Catholic in the old way. Absolutely no one." Or as Anna Quindlen wrote in one of her columns about the Church, "Many of my friends have fled a Catholicism that, for some of us, no longer exists." Brought about in large part by the refusal of Catholics like Quindlen to surrender their place in the pews because of their disagreements with the institutional Church, this transformation does not sit well either with the more traditional faithful or with ex-Catholics who feel vaguely, or sharply, resentful of those who remain inside while picking which requirements to honor and which to ignore. In *The Catholic Myth*, Andrew Greeley describes a television encounter with talk-show host Phil Donahue, in which Donahue, a noisy ex-Catholic, presses Greeley on the issue of faltering Catholic fidelity to the official teachings on birth control, abortion, and celibacy. Come on, Donahue keeps saying, why don't they just be honest with themselves and quit the Church? To which Greeley finally replies, *"Because they like being Catholic."*

For most of the practicing Catholics I interviewed, it is almost that simple. "It's a tradition," said Sally Shea. "I happen to think anyone who is Jewish and doesn't raise his kids Jewish is crazy. The same thing goes for Catholics. Make your own sense out of it. My husband, Danny, is much more ambivalent. When it was time to baptize Kelly, he wasn't wild about it. He has very bad memories of Catholicism and what it meant. I think he had weird nuns, weird priests, who used to slap him around. But I'm not planning to terrorize them with stories of the devil. It's not heavy-duty anymore."

At times it seems as if more Catholics are engaged in a family spat with Holy Mother Church than in practicing their religion—for some, the Church remains too conservative; for others, it has grown too lax—and people tend to pick and choose their parishes with more care than in previous generations. But even as religious vocations and weekly attendance at mass have plummeted, the number of people who call themselves Catholic has remained steady. "I often compare the way I feel about the Church to the way I feel about my country," said John Snyder, a community college professor and father of six grown children who counts himself a liberal Catholic, and who with his wife, Charlene, is deeply involved in the life of the Church. "Many things distress me and I oppose them vehemently, but I love my country."

Similarly, says Anna Quindlen, after her column on

being a cultural Catholic appeared, "I got a lot of mail saying, 'You are *not* a Catholic!' " The ironic counterpoint to such criticism is the effect Quindlen's Catholicism seems to have on many of her professional and social peers. Periodically accused of Catholic-bashing for presuming to question some Church position or other in print, she is just as frequently patronized for being a Catholic herself. "We're 'the Catholics,' " she says, in only partial amusement. "We're trotted out at parties. I remember one dinner party at which I got into a discussion with another woman about *in vitro* conception and she went on about how she thought Catholics must look at the issue and I said, 'Well, we're Catholics,' and she said, 'You mean you *were*,' and I said, 'No, we *are*.' People are just agog."

> "A lot of the Jews I know who are my age are
> like I was—lazy Jews. 'Oh, I'm Jewish, yeah,
> I went to synagogue in 1957, but I haven't
> gone since.' But they eat a knish and you know,
> they're not surprised it's a knish."
>
> —Fred Herschkowitz

The experience of American Jews provides a concentrated lesson in both the precariousness of a religious culture and the tenacity and tentativeness of individual religious identity. Because traditional Jewish law defines as a Jew anyone born of a Jewish mother,* the genetic,

---

*In a defining departure from Orthodoxy, the Reform branch of Judaism, which represents about one-third of American Jews, holds patrilineal descent to be equally legitimate as long as the child is raised in the Jewish tradition.

or ethnic, identification of oneself as a Jew exists as something apart from one's actual religious beliefs or practices. And yet, what that something is, is far from a fixed quantity. To speak of a "Catholic agnostic" or a "nonbelieving Methodist" is an oxymoronic attempt at precision; to speak of a "secular Jew" or a "Jewish atheist" is not implicitly contradictory, however much such terms might offend the genuinely observant. To many people, it seems as if a Jew gets to be a Jew just by being born and, barring conversion, remains one for life.

In interviews with disaffected or nonbelieving gentiles, I was struck by how frequently, and wistfully, this fundamental difference was mentioned. "Jews are lucky," went the curious, ahistoric refrain. "They don't have to throw it all over if they happen not to believe."

While such a reading vastly undervalues the intense and ongoing debate within the Jewish community over what it means to be a Jew, in a practical sense, certainly, it touches on the truth. "If you ask me what my religion is," said David Nichtern, a musician who spent several years as codirector of a Buddhist monastery in Vermont, "I would say I am a Buddhist. But if you ask me where I come from, I would say I am a New York Jew."

Freud, in the preface to the Hebrew translation of *Totem and Taboo*, confessed a similar immutability of identification. "No reader of this book," he wrote, "will find it easy to put himself in the emotional position of an author who is ignorant of the language of Holy Writ, who is completely estranged from the religion of his fathers— as well as from every other religion—and who cannot take a share in nationalist ideals, but who has yet never repudiated his people, who feels that he is in his essential nature a Jew and who has no desire to alter that nature. If the question were put to him: 'Since you have abandoned all these common characteristics of your countrymen, what is there left to you that is Jewish?' he would reply: 'A great deal, and probably its very essence.' "

Of what that essence consists is the subject of inexhaustible discussion among Jews. For every Catholic pointing to someone like Anna Quindlen and fuming, "You are not a Catholic," there is surely one Jew reading Freud out of the family, another nodding in agreement with him, and a third expressing some version of the bewilderment I first heard from Lisa Gallin, whose Jewish-atheist parents sent her and her brothers and sisters to an Orthodox yeshiva in the hope that it would somehow guarantee them a deeply felt Jewish identity. "When I was younger," she said, "I used to think, suppose I was the only Jewish person alive, and I had to reconstruct all the prayers and all the traditions? So I tried to memorize everything, as if its survival depended on me. But now that I'm away from it, I have very mixed feelings. I think about raising my own children as Jews and it's a scary thought. I don't want to have anything to do with it. But if I don't teach my kids, they won't know it—exactly what my parents thought.

"I wish I could say I could take it or leave it," she said, "but it's hard. I really don't know what my Jewish identity is."

For many of the nonbelieving Jews I spoke with, the issue of identity is closely tied up with a sense of allegiance to generations past. Not just to one's own parents or grandparents, but to a long line that stretches back in time to Minsk, to Amsterdam, to Frankfort, to Barcelona—

to Rome, Alexandria, Jerusalem, Auschwitz.* One does not have to be melodramatic to comprehend the sense of obligation to the past that goes with being a Jew, or the burden that such an obligation imposes on the individual. "I'm almost embarrassed to proclaim it," said Mimi Ellis, "but I feel as if to not do it is to write off all those people who held on for centuries, all those people who died because of it. You just cannot walk away from Jewish history."

"How can I do this? How can I not do it?" are frequently paired questions. Or as Nancy Gallin said at one point, after wrestling rhetorically with some of the issues that trouble her about being Jewish, "Who asked for it?"

History, of course, imposes itself on us all, but most of the time, it is easy not to notice. The history of the Jews is ever present, churning out new claims on already oversubscribed consciences, obliging every Jew, in turn, to choose how he will act upon his heritage religiously, politically, culturally. Nobody asks me my opinion of the Irish troubles, or what I make of the dispute between the Vatican and Seattle's Archbishop Hunthausen. But every Jew is expected to have an opinion on the West Bank. One is a Jew whether one likes it or not, and then one has to make up one's mind what to do about it—what kind of a Jew is one to be?

---

*At a dinner party one night, I was talking with an acquaintance I knew to be a nonobservant Jew when the subject of Spanish came up. In mid-sentence, she switched to a flawless, pure Castilian. Where had she learned it, I asked. At home, she said. "Oh, then you grew up in Spain?" "No," she said, "but my family were Sephardim." I hesitated. "The Sephardim were thrown out of Spain in 1492," I said. "That's right," she said, "but my grandmother still spoke it, and my mother. It's what we spoke at home."

"I can't give my children what Mimi wants me to give them," Ronnie McFadden had told me when I interviewed her at her friend Mimi Ellis's suggestion. The two women had become close through their sons, Daniel and Kiya, who were classmates at a neighborhood school. Both women were from nonbelieving Jewish backgrounds, held similar ethical and political views, shared a sense of community and of an individual's obligation to society. Yet each had a fundamentally different conception of what it meant to be Jewish, and of what they owed their children as a result. To McFadden, a college administrator who had just given birth to her second son when I spoke with her, it was truly not an issue. The daughter of "left-wing atheists from Russia," McFadden had been raised "with the idea that anyone really intelligent couldn't be religious. That was my mother's idea," she said wryly. "I'm much more tolerant." Her parents' identity as Jews was nevertheless clear, and so was hers. They were nonreligious Jews with highly developed social consciences. Ellis, on the other hand, had been raised in a family where nonbelief was no obstacle to membership in a synagogue, Hebrew school, or attendance at High Holiday services. They made no pretense of being devout, but neither was the family's observance of tradition unthinkingly undertaken; it represented a conscious desire to maintain continuity with a rich past and a rich culture. It was hard for Mimi to comprehend that such a close friend as Ronnie would not want her children to benefit from the richness of that tradition—or its Christian equivalent, since Ronnie's husband had grown up in a churchgoing Protestant family. "I don't care if it's Jewish or Christian," Ellis argued. "They should have something—a Christmas tree or Hanukkah, something. Kids need celebrations, they need some tradition to be part of."

"Not mine," was McFadden's response. "There are a lot of things I do for my kids as a mother that I would not do on my own. I go to the park, I watch *Sesame Street*, I discuss sports. But giving them a religion I never had is not one of them." Since her husband was himself also a nonbeliever, it seemed equally meaningless to attempt to instruct their sons in some version of the Christian faith. It was the only imaginable choice for them, however puzzling it seemed to Mimi.

In fact, at the time, Ellis and her husband, Howard Mindus, had only recently resolved the question of how deeply to immerse themselves in the Jewish tradition, and it was a decision that had nothing to do with the God in which neither of them believed, but with a particular mix of personal need and historical sentiment. Neither had grown up in a particularly religious home, and except for being married in a Jewish ceremony and occasionally attending High Holiday services with Mimi's parents, neither had had anything to do with formal religion since adolescence. "My parents had parents who were nonbelievers," Mimi says. "It's an old tradition among European Jews."

Yet as the American-born children of German-Jewish refugees, they were conscious not just of how close the world of their parents had come to disappearing but of how small their personal universe was as well—a place bereft of grandparents, cousins, aunts and uncles, of holiday tables with too much elbow room. "We are a very sparse generation," Mimi said. "I didn't know any large families growing up." She, in fact, has one older brother; Howard was an only child. These facts of their lives might not have weighed so heavily if Howard had not been diagnosed with Hodgkin's disease at the age of thirty-six, when their son Daniel was not quite two. Four years later, when Howard suffered a relapse and underwent a second round of treatment, they understood that theirs was going to remain a small family as well. It was impossible to say how long Howard would live, but he would almost certainly die before Daniel grew up, and the twin prospect of facing Howard's death and their diminution as a family afterward started Mimi thinking about the value of a community, of a context, in which to live and die.

Among their close friends at the time were both secular Jews to whom religious observance was alien and unthinkable and as many others who had either never left it behind or had always known they would pick up where their parents had left off once they had children of their own. Some of those children had already begun Hebrew school in anticipation of bar and bat mitzvahs four or five years down the road, and as Daniel turned eight, Mimi realized that they would have to get behind the tradition soon or watch the moment slip by. Howard was not opposed, but he could happily have let it go. For Mimi, as for Jean Kunhardt from a quite different perspective, it came down to not wanting to do things by half measures.

"When I was a child," Mimi recalled, "though we occasionally went to synagogue, we had no ritual in the house. It was typical of my parents and my friends' parents to say—*you* have to go to Hebrew school three times a week but *we* don't do anything. I feel we have to meet Daniel halfway. He is not enthusiastic—he'd rather play baseball, and he has made it clear he is not a believer. But Judaism is a religion of daily life and of law and tradition. That's what I hope to have for us as a family. And I somehow feel that if you don't do this, then in some way you are always an outsider as a Jew."

In the same way she had researched schools for Daniel, and before that, hospitals for Howard, she set out to find a temple where they would be comfortable. "Basically," she says, "you shop for a synagogue. For how liberal you want it to be, for example, or for its ethical emphasis, for how much ritual you are looking for." Having attended a Conservative synagogue as a child, and later coming under the influence of a Reconstructionist rabbi in a nearby town, Mimi knew she wanted to remain within the Conservative movement. Like a number of other nonbelieving Jews I spoke with, both Mimi and Howard viewed the Reform branch of Judaism—which might be thought to have special appeal to nonbelievers—as too spare, too bare bones. "It strikes me," Mimi said, "as having dispensed with too much of what makes religion work in order to accommodate American tastes. It's like having mass in English, I guess. You lose some of the mystery. We wanted a little more of what Howard calls 'smells and bells.' "

They eventually found a Reconstructionist synagogue that was ideologically a good fit, though geographically inconvenient. Daniel began Hebrew school, Mimi volunteered for a committee, and even Howard eventually landed on the financial advisory board, where his skills as a contract lawyer were especially useful. What followed was not on the order of having a child and waking up the next morning to discover life irreversibly transformed, but rather like enrolling in night school and discovering one's perspective imperceptibly changing as the weeks go by. Daniel began to accumulate a private fund of knowledge about Jewish history and traditions, with which he could surprise his parents. Howard actually began to enjoy the occasional service; Mimi grew less self-conscious about having engineered the whole thing. Early on, she had said she was "struggling with how observant to be. We light candles on Friday night, we say blessings over challah. Does it make me feel good? Yes. Do I feel guilty that we don't do more? Sometimes."

A couple of years later, as Howard's final illness stretched into months and became recognizable as the last phase, the choice seemed less arbitrary, more provident. They had not been swept up into some nineteenth-century tableau of a traditional Jewish community, nor had their old friends been supplanted by new friends from the synagogue. Yet what Mimi had hoped for had subtly come about: the family was not marooned in the middle of a cold city as one of life's great passages visited them. In a modest way, they had revived the traditions meant to give shape and order to the life of the family and to anchor it to a larger community. The last few months of Howard's life were like a long siege. He was in the hospital almost continuously from September through January, and then, one Friday afternoon, it was suddenly over. Mimi went to pick up Daniel after school and tell him his father had died. Then they came home and the phone started ringing and friends began arriving. Sometime that evening, Mimi heard Daniel answer the phone and speak to a friend who hadn't yet heard. She heard Daniel tell him that his father had just died and then she heard him say, very calmly, that he was all right. There were a lot of people visiting, he told the friend, and they were preparing to sit *shiva* in Howard's honor. "That's what Jewish people do," he said.

> "We were one of those families you could
> call generic Protestants, It all depended on
> what town we were living in. Sometimes it
> was Congregational, sometimes Episcopal,
> sometimes Methodist."
>
> —Jed Horne

To speak of the contemporary Protestant identity is to invite argument. On the one hand, it is as historically evident as the nose on George Washington's face: America as it used to be, or especially as it liked to think of itself—pious, churchgoing, nonidolatrous—the core of what Harold Bloom calls "the American religion." Constitutional separation of church and state notwithstanding, America was effectively a Protestant country until well into this century. "Protestantism was *the* formative cultural influence," says Daniel Aleshire. "The emergence of Catholic schools in the nineteenth century, for instance, was a clear indication that the public schools were in fact Protestant schools, evidencing a clear anti-Catholic bias." One has only to glance at a McGuffey reader to be reminded of how thoroughly the Protestant ethic and the Protestant perspective once determined the country's cultural standards.

On the other hand, as Protestant theologian Martin E. Marty described it in the winter, 1992, issue of the journal *Religion and American Culture*, "generic" Protestantism is so amorphous a concept at present as to approach meaninglessness. "Protestantism suffers from breadth and vagueness," Marty writes. "Theologically, it is what remains in Western Christianity after one subtracts the

belief of those who live under papal obedience. Socio-
politically, it is the name one uses for a chaos of forces
that have little in common except non-papalism."

In other words, a Protestant is a Christian who is not
a Catholic—the very tautology I picked up in one of those
Catholic grammar schools meant to shelter me from the
de facto Protestant state! To arrive at some meaningful
definition of a given Protestant's religious identity, then,
one must look to the particular denomination. But even
there one runs into trouble. "I may find my identity as
an 'evangelically Catholic Lutheran,' " writes Marty.
"But outside my study or my parish church, I rarely run
across other evangelically Catholic Lutherans in this plu-
ralist and secular society. When I do, I keep some distance
because they are usually writing nasty articles against
slightly different parties of Lutherans."

In the end, remembering Lucy Mack Smith, it may be
that the Protestant self-definition is what most counts,
and it is a definition that has very little to do with official
doctrine or a particular denomination but very much to
do with the satisfaction of frequently competing impulses
toward community and personal spiritual harmony. The
first, it would seem, can only be had by staying put; the
second by moving on. In the hope of reconciling the two,
the majority of Protestants I spoke with described a journey of many stopovers and successive denominational
identifications.

Seeking to explain how she wound up as a member of
a large and thriving suburban Baptist church, Trelawney
Hodge made the point perfectly by beginning with a
description of the very different tradition of her childhood. "I was born to be a Methodist," is how she put

it, recalling a time, place, and tradition that she had left long ago. "All my mother's people were Methodist. My grandfather was a trustee. And in the South when I was growing up, if you were a Methodist, you stayed that way. Even when I went away to college, and started going to a few Baptist churches for the music, I stayed on the rolls of my church back home. I know a lot of men who came to New York years ago, never planning to go back, but they kept on the rolls of their church, just so they could get buried."

It is a recollection of community and habits similar to Wendy Kaufman's, to Candace Burnett's, to Campbell Geeslin's, to Randall Balmer's—church as the center of one's social circle, as one of the guarantors of the local social order, punctuated by clean clothes and Sunday dinner at two o'clock. It was a world, Trelawney observed, that sought to keep things as they were. "In a way, I think it was much the same attitude that helped keep segregation in place for so long. Don't make any changes. Now that they've found out we've become Baptists, it's like, 'How dare you!' "

If she had returned to Florida after college, she might never have changed churches, but after settling in New York, she found her way to the nondenominational Riverside Church, where she and one of her sisters taught in the Sunday school for many years, and where both her sons were baptized, as Methodists. For almost twenty years, it was her religious community as fully as her childhood church had been—and then she moved on again. "What drew me to Riverside originally," she says, "was the beauty of the building, its quiet, medieval quality. But in the summer, when the Sunday school was not in session, I used to go to different Baptist churches for the preaching and the music. Then one time I heard this man preaching on the radio, and I started going to his church up in Mount Vernon, Grace Baptist." In a successful, if unconscious, recreation of the community they once shared, she and her children have since been joined there by her mother and her sister and her children. Everything is different—and the Methodists would be horrified—but in some fundamental way, continuity has been achieved.

That alone seems like a miracle of sorts. In her search for a church, Wendy Kaufman was attempting to satisfy several needs: she wanted a nondogmatic philosophy, she wanted an enlightened Sunday school for her daughter, and she wanted a community. In the Unitarians she found a good philosophic fit, and was not only happy with their Sunday school, but ended up directing it. Yet after three years of deepening involvement in her local Unitarian church, she could not shake the feeling of not quite belonging, of not having become part of a genuine congregation. It was not until she went to Star Island, off the coast of New Hampshire, where the Unitarian-Universalist Church runs seminars for their education staff, that she experienced something like the community she had been seeking. Here was the critical mass of like-minded people willing to dig in. And here she found, for one week in the year, something close to what she had overcome great reluctance to find for herself and her family. "We were all there for the same purpose, which sounds so simple, but it was precisely what I felt was missing from church, where everyone seemed to be seeking their own thing and keeping it a secret. It wasn't consensus I was looking for, but I was not prepared for the lack of clarity about what it is they were doing there, what they believed and what they wanted their children to believe.

"At Star Island there was that clarity. People honored the differences, but they weren't afraid to talk about them, or share what religion meant to them emotionally. They didn't jump back from the questions. There was an enthusiasm for life and for life's big questions—a bravery, and as a result an energy. It had to do with individual conviction—and that's what I found missing in my week-to-week experience."

It is a similar longing for community and moral harmony that continues to draw families to the Methodist camp meeting in Ocean Grove, New Jersey, summer after summer. Founded in 1869, a couple of hundred yards down the boardwalk from Asbury Park, Ocean Grove is a place where parents' convictions about what is best for their children still translate unequivocally into summertime Bible school and choir rather than sleep-away camp or horseback riding, and where the character of private faith is so profoundly internalized as to be, despite generous effort, almost beyond articulation to an outsider.

One drives through the entrance to the town and understands one has left the profane world behind. The shaded streets are quiet and clean, lined with narrow Victorian houses whose porches are arranged with wicker chairs and gliders, flower boxes and hanging plants. This is not the manicured quaintness of a rich summer resort but the tidyness of middle-class rectitude, as scrubbed as a convent parlor. Until a few years ago, when a newspaper delivery service brought successful suit to overturn it, a ban on Sunday driving was firmly enforced, and the town still seems better suited to a pedestrian pace than to the automobiles that transport the growing number of house-holders who are not connected to the camp meeting—weekenders and summer people who value the town's timelessness for aesthetic reasons and have bought their houses from the association that runs both the camp meeting and the surrounding municipality. Some long-time association members have bought year-round houses as well, but the true heart of this seasonal utopia is to be found among the bungalow-style "tents" of white canvas laid out in orderly rows around the soaring Great Auditorium a few blocks in from the ocean.

Neatly trimmed front hedges or rows of potted flowers define imaginary porches beneath striped overhangs in front of each tent. Families come back summer after summer, generation after generation, bearing barbecues and Bibles to summer addresses like "Mt. Zion" or "Mt. Hebron." In the day, the women take the children first to Thornley Chapel for Bible class and arts and crafts, then to the beach. In the evening, children ride their tricycles on the grassy paths, neighbors talk quietly, organ music drifts through the trees from the auditorium. It is a place of children, young mothers, and older couples, of vacationing clergy on busman's holiday. Husbands who aren't in the religion business either commute or arrange to join their families for weekends. Everyone knows everyone else, at least by sight, and although the visiting preachers often preach to small crowds, there is always a waiting list for tents.

In every way it seems a uniquely homogeneous enclave, and I somewhat naïvely assumed that—like properly paid-up Catholics on a pilgrimage to Rome, or a Hadassah group to Israel—the entire encampment would be settled by Methodists-in-good-standing. Instead, I found myself hearing the same litany of congregation-hopping here as I had heard elsewhere. Clearly it was not denominational loyalty that drew these people here but something else.

"I was born a Methodist," went one woman's typical story, "then went to the Presbyterians at the other end of town for a while. Now I'm a Methodist again." "My mother's family were Congregationalists," a woman from Pennsylvania told me, "but my parents took me to the Presbyterian church when I was small. Then when I was eleven, I started going to the Methodist church because of a friend."

Daughters of Methodist ministers explained how they had met and married the sons of Presbyterian elders at Bible college; matriarchs laid out complex denominational genealogies as if tracing blue eyes or a talent for music down through the family tree. For the most part, as elsewhere, these were not ideological or theological defections, but moves of convenience within the larger tradition of a mainstream Protestantism whose outlines have greatly blurred.

For this group of conspicuously serious believers, it was not personal indifference to doctrine that made frequent switching almost a new tradition in itself but an implicit acknowledgment of how the times—and once-immutable institutions—have changed. Whatever religious identity they might be willing to bear allegiance to individually, there remains no institution within the mainstream to demand it, no banner round which to rally.

What does remain is Ocean Grove itself, an informal, low-budget Colonial Williamsburg of small-town Protestantism—America as it once was, or thought itself to be. Here it is possible to invest oneself heart and soul in a way of life that has long since disappeared. Indeed, what one senses here most plainly is not religious fervor but nostalgia for a less confusing time: in a bewildering, and increasingly secular world, Ocean Grove seems a haven of like-mindedness and, more importantly, of continuity.

"I grew up here," a third-generation young woman explained one afternoon. "I was baptized in the auditorium, and so was my daughter. I was Queen of Chapel when I was twelve, sang in the youth choir through college. After I got married, we moved to Georgia, and for two years I didn't come to the Grove. I cried all summer. And when my daughter was born, I realized I couldn't stand her not growing up here. We were on the waiting list for five years, and then we got the same tent my family had when I was a little girl."

The point of "the Grove," as residents call it, lies less in stirring up than in restoring and reassuring. For older residents, the implicit guarantee of the place is that a sermon will sound like a sermon used to. "I come down here to get my batteries charged," is how one resident described it, making clear that the Christianity available elsewhere these days is simply too lukewarm.

"You don't get religion at home," she said. "You get socialism, humanism, the homeless. You never get Jesus anymore." On the other hand, as one longtime resident explained, "When they give the invitation to come down to the altar to accept Christ, it's not like Billy Graham, you know." Of course, Billy Graham is hardly Billy Graham anymore, either, and one could probably find more hand wavers in a charismatic Catholic church than turn up in Ocean Grove during Camp Meeting Week. It isn't that sort of place.

"There are people who come down specially for the

camp meeting and they go to hear a lot of speakers," a second-generation resident said, "but fewer and fewer of the young families go. For us it's more the idea of being here. We come for the people and the feeling of community. People here are not religious fanatics, just committed Christians. We don't sit around talking about religion all day. It's more a sense of community."

What cannot be found, or sustained, at home can be arranged here, at least, year after year, summer after summer, against the flow of time. Not the old-time religion, perhaps, but something close to the memory of it.

Many years ago, Muriel Hall told me, at a time when she thought she had sorted out what she believed from what she had been taught, she was troubled by the difficulty of letting go of all the "trappings" of religion. She didn't believe any of it any longer, she said, yet she was still drawn to it in ways that could not simply be summed up by aesthetics. It was, to her surprise, rather hard to let go, and she confessed what she took to be a weakness to the same friend of her mother's who would later advise her to read the Bible to her children. "What's the matter with me that I can't put it aside?" she asked. "Nothing," the friend replied, 'and went on to describe how, at the close of the pagan era, many of the old Romans had the same problem. Christianity had swept the empire, the emperor had converted, and the people were expected to follow his lead, forgetting the old gods and the old ways. But it was hard to give them up, and "often," said the friend, "at the end of the day, when the light was fading, they would go down to the groves and walk quietly among the trees as their ancestors had before them."

One rainy afternoon a few summers ago, about eight months after her father had died, my daughter and I spent the better part of the afternoon inside an eighth-century Italian church, called San Frediano, in the city of Lucca, about thirty miles from Florence. We were taken there by my friend Gaylen, whose husband, Enrico, grew up in a nearby town. Gaylen and Enrico's nine-year-old son, Neri, was with us, and though he had spent every summer of his childhood in Italy, he had been to church seldom, and was therefore almost as new to the experience as Anna, a recent cathedral veteran and an expert on lighting candles.

San Frediano is a dark Romanesque rectangle, with half-moon shrines to assorted saints lining either side, and just inside the front entrance, a massive baptismal font of pale marble. It is also the reliquary for an obscure thirteenth-century saint, known as Saint Zita, whose preserved body lies in a glass case at a side altar. There are a great many more conventional burial markers in the church as well, but Anna and Neri were transfixed by Saint Zita, and spent twenty minutes or so in her little chapel, staring at her and asking questions about how her body had been preserved in this way, and why. Though ignorant of the science involved, Gaylen and I did our best to explain the idea of veneration—that this was a way people in the "old days" tried to show how much a person's goodness meant to them. Neither of the children seemed frightened or repulsed, but any reverence they felt seemed to have to do with the residual *humanness* of Saint Zita, not her holiness. It was her resemblance to themselves, and her peculiar apparent survival of her own death in this fashion, that interested and confused them. Such an alternative to what both children had recently come to understand to be death's finality appeared to reopen the question of its character in a not unwelcome way. Final isn't the same for everyone, it seemed; not everyone gets put tidily away.

When we were done with Saint Zita, Gaylen and Neri went off to one part of the church, Anna and I to another. When we met up again a bit later, Gaylen said that Neri had a question she thought that I, as a former Catholic, might be able to answer. He wanted to know, she said, whether anybody knows where Jesus is buried. For a moment I was almost comically thrown—"Where *is* he buried?" I thought desperately, as I began scrambling for some lost image of the tomb where his body had been laid. Then I realized that it was not something I'd forgotten but something that had never come up. It had, I realized, never seemed to matter to the story being told. As far as I knew, there was no shrine to mark the place, certainly no basilica like the one Anna and I had just seen at Lourdes.* But I couldn't even come up with a place name, nothing to go with Galilee, Gethsemane, Calvary, Bethlehem, Nazareth. And then it came to me that, of course, the reason I had never cared where Jesus was buried was that it was supposed to have been only temporary. The Resurrection was the whole point, the As-

*A former Methodist I interviewed later that year corrected me gently. There is a basilica in Jerusalem marking Jesus' traditional burial site, and it is called the Holy Sepulchre.

cension its denouement. "No," I finally told Neri, "because he isn't buried anywhere!"

Neri looked predictably puzzled and asked how that could be. He had to be buried somewhere after he was killed, he said. I explained that Catholics and other Christians believe that after Jesus died, his body was taken down from the cross and buried by his mother and his friends nearby, but when they came back to visit three days later, they discovered that he was no longer there, that he had risen from the dead. Later on, Christians believe, he actually rose up into heaven, his body and everything, so that there was nothing of him left here on earth physically. Neri listened very carefully to this explanation, but it clearly made little sense to him, and when I was done, he politely rephrased the question he was interested in getting an answer to. "What I want to know is," he persisted, "if they found Jesus' grave, and they found his bones and everything, would people then know that he was God?"

It was the question of a child raised not on faith or doctrine but on the logic of the natural history museum. It is through their bones, after all, that we know that dinosaurs exist; why shouldn't proof of God be similarly located? And thus were we launched into a discussion of the seen and the unseen. For the next half-hour, surrounded by the artifacts and resonant symbols of one of the most powerful belief systems ever constructed, the four of us sat in the center of the church and entertained a great many of the big questions. We talked about the differences between proof and faith, between knowing and believing, between certainty and hope. Each of the children speculated, in turn, on God's location, and heaven's, on the possibility of knowing God or that he existed, and whether Jesus was God or simply a good person.

Neri said he thought that God had to do with dead people, that only the dead could see him. Anna, who up until then had disavowed all belief in a heaven, geographical or metaphorical, said she thought it might be possible for the Space Shuttle to keep on going, higher and higher, past the moon, and get a look at it. At this, Neri said no, only the dead can get there, establishing heaven as part of a distinct universe in his metaphysics. We then talked about whether the dead can see us even though we can't see them (Anna thought no, Neri thought maybe) and why people want to believe that Jesus is God. The subject of proof cropped up several times more. To Neri's original question about whether discovery of Jesus' bones would prove he was God, I had tried to explain that it would be close to the reverse for devout Christians—that such a discovery would mean he was only a man and not God. But I also felt bound to say that faith, among other things, meant not relying on such proofs. That was the tricky part. You had to decide without certainty. To which Gaylen added, "The truth is, nobody knows. What you two are doing right now is what philosophers have been doing for thousands of years—trying to make sense of things nobody can know for sure. And your ideas make as much sense as anybody else's."

In fact, whatever Neri had been thinking privately, he had very rarely expressed himself so openly on the subject, and his mother, who was raised as an agnostic but had spent a great deal of time as a child going to other people's churches and thinking about their beliefs, was thrilled to discover that he had such a reflective and cu-

rious attitude. Anna, on the other hand, had been spec-
ulating on metaphysical mysteries without letup since she
was three, and what struck me in this context was how,
in the absence of dogma, her ideas continued to evolve.
On the question of heaven, for example, and the consequences of death, I could vouch for a succession of notions
she had come up with independently, as well as for a
succession of opinions she had held on the conventional
answers to the big questions. That this conversation was
taking place at all was due to the fact that neither child
had been raised on metaphysical certainties nor, despite
Neri's baptism in the church of his father's family, in any
coherent religious tradition.

They were, in a sense, inventing their own "myths"
as they went, testing notions that were no more improbable to their logical minds than those represented by the
images or rituals to which their more traditionally tutored
friends were being exposed. Because they were so idiosyncratic, however, it was far from clear whether these
private views would be of help in connecting them to a
larger community or of placing them in the symbolic
stream of Western culture. Our parental delight at being
party to such discourse was tempered by the specter of
dislocation and disconnectedness, and any smugness we
felt at having such wonderfully thoughtful children was
undercut by the same anxiety that besets a parent the first
time he lets his child walk to the corner unaccompanied.
In the end, what we are counting on is that these early
habits of speculation will help them to make sense of the
world, again and again, at different stages of their lives,
in a way that certainty never could, and that if we are at
all lucky, they will reach maturity as secure in the whirl-
wind as they seem now.

Acknowledgments

The best and the only easy part of writing this book was the rich and still unfinished conversation it opened with friends and family. Many of them sat still for formal interviews, but many more worried the subject fervently in my behalf, volunteering opinions about the difficulty of corralling its many parts and contradictions, calling up with suggestions and names of friends to interview, clipping articles, lending books, reporting on overheard conversations and half-remembered dreams. I suspect a few may even have prayed for me, and especially for the book to end, but proper credit for that belongs to my editor, Linda Healey, whose clarity, good judgment, and infinite patience cannot be entirely explained by her years at the Convent of the Sacred Heart. I thank them all, fervently, and also Jennifer Trone, Amanda Urban, and Anna Fay Wainwright, who would prefer to be left out of my next book, unless it's fiction.

A NOTE ON SOURCES

For parents interested in additional reading on one or another of the themes touched on in this book, the following might prove helpful.

RELIGION AND CULTURE

Bloom, Harold, *The American Religion*. New York: Simon & Schuster, 1992.

Campbell, Joseph, *Myths to Live By*. New York: Bantam, 1988.

Dewey, John, *Common Faith*. New Haven, Conn.: Yale University Press, 1934.

Freud, Sigmund, *Civilization and Its Discontents; The Future of an Illusion; Moses and Monotheism; Totem and Taboo*. James Strachey, editor and translator. New York and London: W. W. Norton, 1963.

Greven, Philip, *Spare the Child*. New York: Alfred A. Knopf, 1991.

Hatch, Nathan. *The Democratization of American Christianity*. New Haven, Conn.: Yale University Press, 1989.

Hunter, James Davison, *Culture Wars*. New York: Basic Books, 1991.

James, William, *The Varieties of Religious Experience*. New York: Penguin Books, 1986 ed.

Johnson, Paul, *A History of Christianity*. New York: Atheneum, 1976.

———, *A History of the Jews*. New York: Harper & Row, 1987.

Jung, C. G. *Psychology and Western Religion*. Princeton, N. J.: Bollingen Series, Princeton University Press, 1984.

Warner, Marina, *Alone of All Her Sex: The Myths and the Cult of the Virgin Mary*. New York: Alfred A. Knopf, 1983.

Wills, Garry, *Under God*. New York: Simon & Schuster, 1990.

RELIGION AND CHILDREN

Bell, Martin, *The Way of the Wolf.* New York: Ballantine Books, 1968.

Fowler, James W., *Stages of Faith.* San Francisco: Harper & Row, 1981.

Heller, David, *Talking to Your Child About God.* New York: Bantam, 1988.

Kushner, Harold S., *When Bad Things Happen to Good People.* New York: Avon, 1981.

———, *Who Needs God?* New York: Summit, 1989.

Meissner, William, *Psychoanalysis and Religious Experience.* New Haven, Conn., and London: Yale University Press, 1984.

Rizzuto, Anna-Maria, *The Birth of the Living God.* Chicago: University of Chicago Press, 1979.

MIXED MARRIAGE

Cowan, Paul and Rachel, *Mixed Blessings.* New York: Penguin, 1988.

SOCIAL AND MORAL DEVELOPMENT

Bettelheim, Bruno. *A Good Enough Parent.* New York: Alfred A. Knopf, 1987.

———, *The Uses of Enchantment.* New York: Vintage Books, 1977.

Coles, Robert, *The Moral Life of Children.* Boston: The Atlantic Monthly Press, 1986.

———, *The Spiritual Life of Children.* Boston: Houghton Mifflin Company, 1990.

Duska, Ronald, and Mariellen Whelan, *Moral Development.* New York: The Paulist Press, 1975.

Erikson, Erik H., *Childhood and Society.* New York: W. W. Norton, 1950, 1963.

Leach, Penelope, *Your Baby and Child,* New York: Alfred A. Knopf, 1982.

———, *Your Growing Child,* New York: Alfred A. Knopf, 1986.

Schulman, Michael and Eva Mekler, *Bringing Up a Moral Child.* Reading, Mass.: Addison-Wesley, 1985.

Spock, Benjamin, *Baby and Child Care.* New York: Pocket Books, 1981.

———, *Dr. Spock on Parenting.* New York: Simon & Schuster, 1988.

Winnicott, D. W., *Playing and Reality.* London and New York: Routledge, 1990.

PERSONAL REFLECTION

Balmer, Randall, *Mine Eyes Have Seen the Glory.* New York: Oxford University Press, 1989.

Quindlen, Anna, *Living Out Loud.* New York: Ballantine Press, 1988.

Russell, Betrand, *Why I Am Not a Christian.* New York: Touchstone Press, 1967.